shouting at Jesus

Unleash an Impolite Faith

D1559912

Matthew Hartsfield

Shouting at Jesus: Unleash an Impolite Faith
Copyright © 2012 by Matthew Hartsfield

Requests for information should be addressed to:

Matthew Hartsfield
17030 Lakeshore Road
Lutz, FL 33558
www.MatthewHartsfield.com

Library of Congress Cataloging-in-Publication Data

Shouting at Jesus / Matthew Hartsfield.

> p. cm. – Inspirational
> Includes bibliographical references.
> ISBN 978-0-9849583-0-6 (pbk.)

LCCN #2011963561

Printed in the United States of America

DEDICATION

To my wife, Maisie.

Your abundant encouragement and unwavering faith made this book a reality.

PREFACE

Dear Reader,

You may have known Jesus for years. You're a veteran believer like me. But like me, does your faith sometimes run dry? Are there moments when intensity fades and expectations diminish? Even when you're faithfully following Jesus you might need to shake off the cobwebs and get out of the ruts of a safe faith. Remember the definition of insanity? It's doing the same thing over and over and expecting different results.

Or you may be rookie believer. You've just begun your journey with Jesus. But you might have surrendered to Jesus on your own terms. You may be following a script that's merely about sin management and moral improvement, not abundant life. You play by the rules and do your part and you expect God to play by the rules and do his part. You may be already be playing it safe and stunting your faith.

Maybe you went to church as a kid, but drifted away later in life. Or you went to church for years but something happened. You got disillusioned, probably hurt or disappointed. It might have happened all at once or just a slow drain over time. Did Jesus just fade for you and gradually move into the background of your life?

You might have only been to church for a wedding or a funeral. You've wondered about Jesus and have been a casual observer from a distance. You've had your doubts, your skepticism and your criticisms. And maybe Jesus has been attractive to you but you've had problems with how church works.

Regardless of your status, this book is for you! Wherever you are in your relationship with Jesus, it's time to start enjoying the great adventure he wants you to experience with him. It's time to start doing life with Jesus on his terms. It's time to unleash your faith. You do life with real problems, real pains, real fears, real hopes and real dreams. It's time you started doing real life with a real God!

CONTENTS

Preface...i

An Amazing Introduction...1

Stop Being So Polite!...5

Shout Over the Noise 17

Go Climb a Tree 27

Dig a Hole 37

Scream in the Storm 49

Start Begging.. 59

Claw Through Crowds... 69

Sneak Through Darkness 81

Keep On Asking 89

Push Beyond Boundaries 97

Go Against All Odds... 105

Run Through Rejections... 115

Closing Challenge... 123

Appendix 125

AN AMAZING INTRODUCTION

"O People of God, be great
believers! Little faith will bring your
souls to heaven, but great faith will
bring heaven to your souls."
Charles Spurgeon

Some people hung on his every word, while others wanted to throw him off a cliff. Some reacted to his powers with joy, and others accused him of being an agent of the Devil. Sometimes they picked up palm branches to wave at him, and sometimes they picked up rocks to stone him. While some were planning to crown him King, others were plotting to kill him. The same crowd that shouted *"Hosanna!"* would soon be shouting, *"Crucify him!"* There was never a dull moment with Jesus.

When I explore the gospels I notice one word in particular that was constantly used to describe people's reactions to Jesus: *"amazed!"* The crowds were *"amazed"* at his teaching (Matthew 7:28, Mark 5:20). The disciples were *"amazed"* at his ability to calm the wind and waves (Matthew 8:27, Mark 6:51). The people were *"amazed"* when he drove out demons

(Matthew 12:23, Mark 1:22). Crowds were *"amazed"* when they saw the lame walk, the blind see, and the deaf hear (Matthew 15:31, Mark 7:37).

In the second chapter of Mark's gospel we are told the story of a paralyzed man who was lowered through a hole in the roof to receive healing from Jesus. As soon as he was healed he got up, picked up his mat, and walked right out of the crowded room of stunned onlookers. Mark said: *"This <u>amazed</u> everyone and they praised God, saying, 'We've never seen anything like this!'"* (Mark 2:12b NIV).

I'm not content to simply read those pages in Scripture. I want to experience that myself! I want to have encounters with Jesus that leave me breathlessly exclaiming, "I've never seen anything like that!" I want to be constantly amazed by Jesus.

> I want to have encounters with Jesus that leave me breathlessly exclaiming, "I've never seen anything like that!"

And here's where it gets personal. Jesus is also amazed by me! That's right. You and I have the ability to amaze Jesus. We learn from the gospels that people amazed Jesus as much as he amazed them. This, however, is both good news and bad news.

On one hand, Jesus was amazed at the bold belief of some people. In Luke's gospel we hear about a Roman officer who approached Jesus seeking healing for his slave. After an amazing display of faith by the officer, Luke says: *"When Jesus heard this, he was <u>amazed</u>. Turning to the crowd, he said, 'I tell you, I haven't seen faith like this in all the land of Israel!'"* (Luke 7:9).

On the other hand, Jesus was amazed at some people's unbelief. When Jesus was rejected in his hometown of Nazareth, Mark writes: *"And because of their unbelief, he couldn't do any mighty miracles among them except to place his hands on a few sick people and heal them. And he was <u>amazed</u> at their unbelief"* (Mark 6:5–6).

We will always be amazing to Jesus. But the choice is ours as to how we will amaze him. We get to choose the attitude by which we approach Jesus. We get to set the expectation for our encounters with him.

> We will always be amazing to Jesus. But the choice is ours as to how we will amaze him.

I never want Jesus to be amazed at my unbelief. I shudder at the thought of Mark, or anyone, saying: "And because of Matthew Hartsfield's unbelief, Jesus couldn't do any mighty miracles in his life." Who would want to be described like the unfaithful town of Nazareth? I want to be known like the Roman officer.

I want Jesus to look at me, amazed by my belief, and exclaim, "Wow! I haven't seen faith like Matthew's in all of Tampa Bay!"

Jesus longs to move in our lives in powerful and miraculous ways. He loves seeing our souls filled with high-expectation faith, anxiously coming to him with all that's on our hearts. Jesus wants to bring healing to our hurt, peace to our pain and clarity to our confusion. He deeply desires a bold and sincere approach, believing, against all odds, that he can do wonders in our lives.

I hope the stories in this book will ignite your faith in Jesus and embolden your relationship with him. The Bible teaches us how wild, untamed and raw our faith needs to be when we come to Jesus. Let these Jesus-encounters touch your heart with a desire to run into his arms, shouting out with all your might to a loving God who is amazed by you!

1.

STOP BEING SO POLITE!

From our earliest childhood days we are taught to be polite. We are told to mind our manners and observe certain social graces:

- Say "please" and "thank you"
- Don't interrupt
- Be patient
- Use your "inside voice"
- Don't make a scene
- Don't whine
- Don't nag
- Stay in your place
- Don't be demanding

My wife, Maisie, and I certainly did all we could to make sure our daughters, Sarah and Jill (now young women), were raised to be nice and polite. We are proud of the fact that Sarah's first words were *"Dank Du,"* her first attempt to say *"Thank You."* Isn't that sickeningly sweet?

Certainly we need to be polite, kind and gracious to each other. Our contemporary culture is in desperate need of manners. Simple politeness serves as a lubricant in a world moving at an increasingly fast pace. We can all tell stories of people who have been rude to us in traffic, at work, while shopping and even at church. Especially at church! Manners have become such a rare commodity that any display of politeness stands out in stark contrast to the rest of our day.

Christians, in particular, are expected to lead mannerly, polite lives. We are challenged to be gracious, kind and loving to all—*"turning the other cheek"* (Matthew 5:39, Luke 6:29) and *"praying for our enemies"* (Matthew 5:44). In fact, an old phrase is still used sometimes in our culture when someone does something nice for someone. People say: "That's very Christian of you." This phrase is often applied regardless of any knowledge of the person's actual faith in Christ. It's just that Christians are expected to personify politeness.

> I know, it seems odd and counter-intuitive, but being too polite can hinder our relationship with Jesus, diminish our faith, and handicap our prayers.

This expectation of politeness, however, can have a damaging effect on our spiritual development. I know, it seems odd and counter-intuitive, but being too polite can hinder our relationship with Jesus, diminish our faith, and handicap our prayers. Let me explain.

Most Christians maintain a very "polite" faith. We tend to cultivate a controlled and managed relationship with Jesus. We treat Jesus politely and we expect the same from him. We are going to stay in our place and we expect Jesus to stay in his place. We won't expect too much from him and we hope he doesn't expect too much from us. We sing safe songs, pray safe prayers and preach safe sermons. Our relationship with God is simply safe and polite.

However, when I explore the Bible, I encounter an untamed God who refuses to be confined to a box of people's safe expectations. The Scriptures reveal a fiercely wild, bold and powerful God who often tosses "politeness" aside in search of a genuine and authentic relationship with his people. God longs to have a relationship with you that pushes your faith to the limits, tests your courage and emboldens your prayers.

Are you trying to have a tame relationship with our untamable God? We often do this because we still want to call the shots and at least maintain an illusion of control in our lives.

> Are you trying to have a tame relationship with our untamable God?

When we are under this illusion of control we convince ourselves that we don't have to be desperate for God—we don't have to depend on him. Most followers of Jesus fall into this "safe" faith that doesn't get out of line or expect too much. Instead of receiving all the fullness of God, we settle for so much less. We offer up our orderly, nice prayers and we certainly don't want to be impolite when we approach God.

Try as I might, I can't find this notion in the Bible. God expects us to approach him with a sense of raw urgency that couldn't care less about proper words or polite formulas. People of faith in the Bible—people who touched the heart of God—were desperately aware of their dependence on him and refused to play little games with him. They refused to operate by a preconceived set of "rules" about interacting with God in a safe and polite fashion.

The Psalms consistently demonstrate this dynamic interaction with God. Psalm 42 sums up the heart of this urgent seeking of God's heart.

> *As the deer pants for streams of*
> *water, so I long for you, O God. I*
> *thirst for God, the living God. When*
> *can I go and stand before him?*
>
> Psalm 42:1,2

When was the last time you had that kind of passion for running into the arms of God and pouring your heart out to him? When was the last time you were that hungry and thirsty for a display of God's presence in your life?

David, the shepherd-boy turned king, was certainly one of these raw and urgent believers who threw politeness out the window when it came to relating to God! His Psalms show an insistent, demanding, often impolite pleading:

> *O Lord, oppose those who oppose*
> *me. Declare war on those who are*
> *attacking me. Put on your armor,*
> *and take up your shield. Prepare*
> *for battle, and come to my aid.*
>
> Psalm 35:1,2

These verses are even more striking when para-phrased by Eugene Peterson in *The Message* Bible:

> *Harass these hecklers, God,*
> *punch these bullies in the nose.*
> *Grab a weapon, anything at*
> *hand; stand up for me!*
>
> Psalm 35:1,2

Now that doesn't sound very polite to me! Is that what your prayer time sounded like today! In fact, it could be called downright rude. David wasn't afraid to be demanding. David wasn't shy about pouring out his heart to God. David certainly wasn't timid about his gut-wrenching prayer language. He knew he could count on God, and God alone, to come through for him.

Just look at some of David's other prayers as
rendered by Eugene Peterson in *The Message* Bible:

> *Don't turn a deaf ear when I call*
> *you, God. If all I get from you is*
> *deafening silence, I'd be better off*
> *in the Black Hole. I'm letting you*
> *know what I need, calling out for*
> *help and lifting my arms toward*
> *your inner sanctum.*
> Psalm 28:1,2 (MSG)

> *Listen, God! Please pay attention!*
> *Can you make sense of these*
> *ramblings, my groans and cries?*
> *King-God, I need your help. Every*
> *morning you'll hear me at it again.*
> *Every morning I lay out the pieces*
> *of my life on your altar and*
> *watch for fire to descend.*
> Psalm 5:1–3 (MSG)

> *Generous in love—God, give grace!*
> *Huge in mercy—wipe out my bad*
> *record. Scrub away my guilt, soak*
> *out my sins in your laundry.*
> Psalm 51:1,2 (MSG)

Should we criticize David for being rude in his
prayers? Or should we remind ourselves that David
was described by God as *"a man after my own*

heart" (Acts 13:22). God and David had an intense relationship with each other and God certainly showed up in powerful ways throughout David's life. It was a relationship fueled, in David's heart, by deep passion and high-expectation faith in his God. David was so exuberant in his relationship with God that he was willing to make a fool of himself by dancing before the Lord to show his pleasure over the Ark's return to Jerusalem. He was so excited that in his high-kicking dance he inadvertently exposed himself! (Obviously this was no slow dance.) He said to his critical wife, Michal, *"...I am willing to act like a fool in order to show my joy in the Lord. Yes, I am willing to look even more foolish than this..."* (2 Samuel 6:21,22 TLB). Are you willing to be a fool for God?

This type of high-expectation interaction can be found throughout the Old Testament in people like Abraham, Sarah, Isaac, Moses, Deborah, Elijah, Joshua and a host of others. This questionable cast of characters played powerful roles in the redemptive drama played out in the pages of Scripture. Like David, they were imperfect and even made some huge mistakes. But they had a deep hunger for God and a passionate desire to run to him and throw caution to the wind as they pleaded their case before him. These were people who wouldn't be content with anything less than God's best!

Ultimately, God decided to take his desire to build these dynamic relationships with us to a whole new level. He came to earth himself in the form of his Son, Jesus Christ. This was the perfect display of a wild and untamed God who will not conform to the safe and polite boxes we construct for him.

Jesus was born to an obscure, poor couple in a filthy stable and laid in an unsanitary, stinking feeding trough. He came at an inconvenient time in the middle of an inconvenient trip for his parents, with no regard for their comfort. He made it a difficult night for an innkeeper and for the animals in the stable. God didn't send an announcement of his birth to either the Roman or Hebrew authorities. Instead the angels made an abrupt and dramatic announcement to the shepherds that almost sent them into coronary arrest. Jesus simply showed up and changed everything. Not a very polite way to start world redemption!

Throughout the gospels Jesus rattled the cages of those who wanted to keep God in a box. The religious hierarchy of the day didn't know what to do with such a raw and untamed God who would not be "polite." They didn't know what to do with a God they couldn't control and manage. So, in their feeble attempts to make God safe, they ended up crucifying him. They missed out on the greatest offer of human history because they were looking for a polite God they could respond to in a safe way.

The people that actually allowed their hearts to be touched by Jesus, however, didn't always fit the mold of "nice Christians." The people who experienced all of God's best were at times loud, rude and obnoxious.

> The people who experienced all of God's best were at times loud, rude and obnoxious.

They simply wouldn't let anything or anyone get in the way. Nothing could stand between them and Jesus. Throwing caution to the wind, they were going to connect with God in a powerful way and plead their case. They weren't going to settle for less.

These people overcame all obstacles to get close to Jesus. They went beyond the norm and ran into the arms of God with a "whatever it takes" brand of faith. They used unconventional methods and made many people uncomfortable along the way. They simply refused to take "No" for an answer. These were people who were willing to move beyond a polite faith and even shout at Jesus to get his attention!

Take a look at the odd assortment of real people and parable characters presented to us in the gospels. Their pictures should appear whenever we search the dictionary for the words, "impolite," "rude" and "loud":

- Blind Bartimaeus was willing to shout at Jesus above the noise of the disapproving crowd telling him to shut up. (Mark 10:46–52)

- Zaccheus was willing to rise above the obstacles that prevented him from seeing Jesus, even if it meant climbing a tree! (Luke 19:1–10)

- The paralytic and his four friends were willing to be so rude as to rip a hole in someone's roof to get to Jesus. (Mark 2:1–12)

- The bleeding woman was willing to rudely—and we might add illegally—claw her way through the crowd to touch Jesus. (Luke 8:40–56)

- The disciples themselves were willing to scream at Jesus while he was taking a nap! (Mark 4:35–41)

- The persistent widow was willing to be a rude beggar to have her case heard. (Luke 18:1–8)

- The unrelenting, rude neighbor was willing to knock on a locked door until his knuckles were bleeding to get bread. (Luke 11:6–8)

- Martha was willing to read Jesus the riot act in order to show her fears and frustrations to him. (John 11)

- Nicodemus was willing to sneak around under the cover of night and disturb Jesus to pursue truth. (John 3:1–9)

- The Gentile woman was willing to nag Jesus to get her child healed. (Mark 7:24–30)

- Jairus was willing to risk great social embarrassment to see his daughter made well. (Luke 8:40–56)

- The Roman officer was willing to move beyond accepted social barriers to bring healing to his slave. (Luke 7:2–10)

- The untouchable leper was willing to risk his life to get close to Jesus. (Matthew 8:1–3)

- Parents were ready to fight with the disciples to get their children blessed by Jesus. (Matthew 19:13–15)

Jew and Gentile, rich and poor, educated and uneducated, men and women. It didn't matter. All that mattered was their unquenchable desire to get to Jesus. They didn't care how foolish they looked or how impolite they had to be on their mission. They would endure anything for the sake of having a one-on-one encounter with Jesus.

These are the people who thrilled the heart of Jesus. He loved their foolishness. He marveled at their persistence. He was amazed by their faith. It melted his heart to see these people so desperate to receive his touch. These are the kind people that move the heart of God! Don't you want to be one of these people?

In the chapters ahead we will further explore some of these impolite encounters. These little stories of amazingly impolite faith will challenge and inspire your faith. Let these chapters become a guide to developing a rude and raw faith—the kind of faith that changes your life and changes the world. See what it's like to unleash your faith. Learn how to start shouting at Jesus!

2.

SHOUT OVER THE NOISE

*Then they reached Jericho, and as
Jesus and his disciples left town, a
large crowd followed him. A blind
beggar named Bartimaeus (son of
Timaeus) was sitting beside the road.
When Bartimaeus heard that Jesus
of Nazareth was nearby, he began
to shout, "Jesus, Son of David, have
mercy on me!" "Be quiet!" many of
the people yelled at him. But he only
shouted louder, "Son of David, have
mercy on me!" When Jesus heard him,
he stopped and said, "Tell him to come
here." So they called the blind man.
"Cheer up," they said. "Come on, he's
calling you!" Bartimaeus threw aside
his coat, jumped up, and came to
Jesus. "What do you want me to do for
you?" Jesus asked. "My rabbi,"
the blind man said, "I want to see!"
And Jesus said to him, "Go, for your
faith has healed you." Instantly the
man could see, and he followed
Jesus down the road.*

Mark 10:46–52

Crowds. They were a constant condition of Jesus' travels. The crowds were composed of curiosity seekers, skeptics and a few sincere followers. Mark tells us this particular crowd was large. There must have been a circus atmosphere surrounding Jesus' departure from town that day. It was basically a parade, and poor Bartimaeus had the worst seat.

But what did that matter to him? He couldn't see anyway. Bartimaeus always seemed to be on the fringe of life. He was forced to beg for a living and was shunned by many who considered his blindness a curse from God (Leviticus 26:14–16). Bartimaeus seemed destined to spend the rest of his life in the dark, begging for mere survival.

But not today! Today would be different. Today could change everything. Today, Jesus was nearby! Bartimaeus had heard the stories about this amazing Rabbi from Nazareth. He had heard about the lame walking, the deaf hearing and the blind seeing. Were they just stories? Was Jesus really from God? Why should Bartimaeus get his hopes up? It wasn't worth the disappointment. Or was it?

As Jesus was passing by, something bubbled up from a deep place in Bartimaeus' soul—something he hadn't felt in years. Hope! Surely the stories were true. Surely this Jesus was actually the Messiah. Bartimaeus couldn't miss this golden opportunity. From his place on the fringe in the back of the crowd he could never navigate his way to Jesus. He couldn't see, and certainly no one would help him. By the time he got there, Jesus would have been long gone.

Bartimaeus cleared his throat, filled his lungs with the dusty air and gave a shout that pierced the noisy crowd surrounding Jesus. *"Jesus, Son of David, have mercy on me!"* (Mark 10:47). It was a shout of faith! It was a shout that left no doubt he believed. In referring to Jesus as the "Son of David," he was basically calling him Messiah.

But to the crowd it was just plain rude. How dare Bartimaeus ruin this moment for them. Couldn't he shut up and stop begging for a few moments? They were embarrassed for Bartimaeus and for themselves. Why would he be so forward as to shout at the Rabbi? They tried to silence him. They tried to put him in his place. They tried to remind him he was a mere beggar, destined for destruction. Stop hoping Bartimaeus. Stop dreaming. Stop believing.

Bartimaeus would have none of it. This day he wouldn't listen to the crowd. He wouldn't believe the worst about himself. He wouldn't be satisfied with anything less than the very touch of Jesus. He reared back, took an even deeper breath and shouted louder than before. And this time Jesus stopped. He called for Bartimaeus. The curious onlookers relayed the news to Bartimaeus that Jesus asked to see him.

Bartimaeus wasted no time. He threw off his cloak. He didn't want anything slowing him down on his way to Jesus. But as soon as he arrived, Jesus asked a very curious question, "What do you want me to do for you?" Forgive me, but it seems like a stupid question. Wasn't it obvious what Bartimaeus wanted and needed? Did he need to spell it out for Jesus?

But Jesus wanted to hear it directly from his lips. Jesus wanted Bartimaeus to declare to him and to the crowd, exactly what he wanted. He wanted to know how focused Bartimaeus was about what he expected from Jesus. Bartimaeus was a high-expectation believer and he had no problem answering that question. *"I want to see!"* And most amazing of all, Jesus rewards his amazingly rude faith and gives Bartimaeus new vision. He can see!

Believing for More than You Can See

What about you? Have you ever felt like Bartimaeus? Sure, you may have your sight, but something's missing. It feels like you are on the fringe. You have limitations, real or perceived, that hold you back. You've got hurts, habits or hang-ups that keep you from the life you always imagined. Have you settled for less? Are you content with the way you've been defined by others? Are you content with the way you've defined yourself?

There's no reason to be left in the dark—blind to the amazing potential that God has placed in you. Bartimaeus believed God had something more for him. He believed there was something beyond the darkness. While he was still blind, he had hope. He had faith. He could believe for more than he could see.

Do you believe God has something more for you? Do you believe God has a future, a direction and a vision for your life? Start shouting! Nothing happened until Bartimaeus started shouting. When he put his hope into action and called out to Jesus, his life began to change dramatically. He wasn't quite sure what would happen, or how it would take place. But that didn't' matter. All he had to do was the possible. He would let Jesus take care of the impossible.

Do you believe God has something more for you?

Don't Stop Shouting

Bartimaeus came very close to missing his miracle that fateful day. After his first shout to Jesus, the crowd tried to silence him. They tried to keep him in his place and dash his hopes. He could very easily have listened to the crowd. He could have been polite. But which was louder—the external noise of negativity or the inward hope that was screaming to be heard? All too often we let the noise of everything around us convince us we should just give in, give up or give out. It took raw courage for Bartimaeus to keep on shouting. He was risking everything. The crowd he was upsetting was the same crowd he relied on each day as a beggar. How could he afford to alienate these people?

Even though he couldn't see yet, he kept a steely focus on Jesus, took the risk and shouted even louder. Notice, Jesus didn't stop after the first shout, but he did take notice after Bartimaeus kept shouting. Jesus loves to see faith like that. He is thrilled with an enduring heart and an irrepressible hope. If we learn anything in the pages ahead we'll see that Jesus loves the persistent heartbeat of hope in us. He loves to reward a faith that keeps on believing!

Move Quickly When He Calls

Notice as well that when Jesus called for Bartimaeus he threw off his cloak and came as quickly as possible. He wanted to remove any barriers or restrictions that kept him from getting to Jesus as soon as possible. Are you willing to cast off anything that gets in the way? When Jesus calls do you move as quickly as possible?

The writer of Hebrews speaks very clearly about this:

*...let us strip off every weight that
slows us down, especially the sin
that so easily trips us up.
And let us run with endurance the
race God has set before us.*
Hebrews 12:1b

It's not always easy to leave our comfort zones and embark on new adventures with Jesus. We get used to the excess weight that slows down our lives. Many people don't realize the self-defeating habits that stall their lives and create a drag on their ability to *"run the race"* that Jesus is inviting us to join.

What Do You Want?

Jesus asked Bartimaeus, *"What do you want me to do for you?"* I used to think that was one of the most unnecessary questions in the Bible. Why would Jesus bother to ask the obvious? Now I see that question as central to my life. It is one of the most important questions ever asked of any human being. And Jesus is asking you that question as well, *"What do you want me to do for you?"*

Jesus wanted Bartimaeus to be very clear about his needs and desires. Jesus is looking for a sense of focus in our faith. That means I need to look at the good and bad of my life and realize what I desperately need from Jesus. Go ahead, take a time-out and think about what you would say if Jesus were standing face to face with you and asked, *"What do you want me to do for you?"* How would you respond? Where do you need God to show up in a big way in your life right now?

Where do you need God to show up in a big way in your life right now?

Some of us are too polite when asked questions like that. We feel we shouldn't really ask for anything for ourselves. We should put ourselves last. Shouldn't we be like a "Miss America" contestant and just ask for "world peace?" Really?! Bartimaeus didn't hesitate for even a second. He was very well aware of his inadequacies and shortcomings. He was very clear about the impossible situation he faced every day. He knew exactly what he needed Jesus to do that was beyond his own abilities.

Make a list. Get focused. Get ready to respond to Jesus' question. He's asking it right now. He wants to know where you really need his touch, his healing, his power and direction in your life. Bartimaeus didn't measure his words, he didn't stop and wonder about it for a while, saying: "Just hang on a second Jesus and let me think that over." No, he was ready. Are you?

Your Next Step

Bartimaeus' restored sight gave him new freedom. He could go anywhere and do anything. He could use his sight any way he wanted. Jesus didn't put conditions on his healing. Jesus didn't pledge to revoke it if he didn't do the right thing with his new eyes. So what does Bartimaeus do with his new-found freedom? He follows Jesus.

Bartimaeus' first steps as a sighted person are to walk in the footsteps of his healer. Luke tells us *"he followed Jesus down the road."* He didn't know where the road would lead. He didn't know exactly where Jesus was going or what was about to happen. But none of that mattered. He just wanted to be with Jesus and be counted among his followers. Those were amazing first steps that continued to demonstrate his love, loyalty and faith for Jesus. Jesus is looking for your next steps as well.

3.

GO CLIMB A TREE

Jesus entered Jericho and made his way through the town. There was a man there named Zacchaeus. He was the chief tax collector in the region, and he had become very rich. He tried to get a look at Jesus, but he was too short to see over the crowd. So he ran ahead and climbed a sycamore-fig tree beside the road, for Jesus was going to pass that way. When Jesus came by, he looked up at Zacchaeus and called him by name. "Zacchaeus!" he said. "Quick, come down! I must be a guest in your home today." Zacchaeus quickly climbed down and took Jesus to his house in great excitement and joy. But the people were displeased. "He has gone to be the guest of a notorious sinner," they grumbled. Meanwhile, Zacchaeus stood before the Lord and said, "I will give half my wealth to the poor, Lord, and if I have cheated people on their taxes, I will give them back four times as much!" Jesus responded, "Salvation has come to this home today, for this man has shown himself to be a true son of Abraham. For the Son of Man came to seek and save those who are lost."

Luke 19:1–10

Zacchaeus had what most people want—money and power. By all accounts he was a very successful man. Money was coming in almost faster than he could count. He knew all the right people in all the right places. And nobody wanted to mess with him because, as a tax-collector for the Roman Empire, he had Roman soldiers at his disposal to deal with any delinquent taxpayers.

But something was missing—something he couldn't buy with his money or attain with his power. He couldn't quite put his finger on it, but something had to change. There was a growing hole in his soul that couldn't be filled with anything he possessed. Despite his full rolodex, Zacchaeus was likely lonely, with no real friends. He was regarded a traitor and a thief by his own people. He, like his colleagues, would overcharge people and line his own pockets while the Roman authorities looked the other way. His lifestyle had isolated him and it was beginning to take its toll.

He may also have noticed how much guilt—which until now he had been able to suppress—was bubbling up to the surface with increasing regularity. It would have haunted him and gnawed at him, making it difficult to sleep or find any real peace in his life. He was in a downward spiral with no way out.

But Jesus was coming to town. Like Bartimaeus, Zacchaeus had heard the stories of this remarkable Rabbi. He knew that people who encountered Jesus were experiencing radical life change. When people had a real one-on-one with Jesus, they were never the same. Zacchaeus began to feel an adrenaline rush like he hadn't felt in years. Maybe, just maybe, Jesus could change everything. He had to see Jesus!

> Maybe, just maybe, Jesus could change everything. He had to see Jesus!

But Zacchaeus had to rise above some obstacles before he could see Jesus. He was "vertically challenged." By the time he got to the place where Jesus would be passing, a large crowd already lined the road. There was no way he could see over the much taller heads. Desperation began to creep into his spirit. He had to do something. He had to see Jesus. But he couldn't jump high enough to take a peek and no one would give up their spot on the "parade route."

To surmount this obstacle he had to clear another hurdle, his pride. Zacchaeus spotted a sycamore tree close to the road. But he was a man of power and riches. It was beneath him to shimmy up a tree like a monkey. But none of that mattered now. He was willing to cast aside whatever was left of his dignity and get up that tree. So he clamored up the tree and perched himself on a limb just in time to see Jesus make his approach.

His pulse was racing and his heart was about to pop out of his chest. And then Jesus did the unexpected. He stopped! He looked straight up into the tree and called out to Zacchaeus. He told him to get down immediately. He wanted to be a guest in Zacchaeus' home that day. Unbelievable! Jesus had not only noticed him but wanted to hang out with him!

Zacchaeus' head was spinning, but he didn't hesitate for even a second. He probably looked more foolish than when he climbed up in the first place. Getting down from trees safely can be little trickier than getting up. He couldn't remember the last time he felt so excited. But he didn't care what he looked like. He wasn't letting anything or anyone get in his way.

But people tried to get in his way. The stunned crowd shook their heads in disbelief and disgust. They couldn't accept that Jesus wanted to go to the house of this cheating, thieving, sinning tax-collector. They made their contempt known, but for Zacchaeus it was like they didn't even exist. This little tree-climber had locked eyes with God and no one was going to steal this moment of life-changing joy.

Claiming Jesus as Lord, Zacchaeus then said something that was even more shocking. He was a new man and he was going to give evidence of his changed life. He would give half his riches to the poor and he would repay anyone he had ever overcharged, four times over. Now that's a tax rebate! He was absolutely delirious with his new-found relationship with Jesus and it affected everyone around him.

Jesus responded by assuring salvation for Zacchaeus and his home, reaffirming how lost Zacchaeus had been. Jesus used this as an opportunity to remind everyone of his mission—to seek and save the lost.

It Doesn't Matter Who You Are

Zacchaeus and Bartimaeus were 180 degrees removed from each other. One had everything and the other had nothing. One was on top of his game and the other was a miserable beggar. Both, however, needed the same thing. They needed Jesus. It doesn't matter what you have or don't have if you don't have a relationship with Jesus.

By all outward appearances Zacchaeus had it made. But, when he did an internal audit of his soul, he realized how broke he was. What does it look like inside your soul? Look beyond the outer trappings and see what's missing. Are you experiencing the joy, peace and purpose in your life that God has always intended for you? Don't be fooled by the world's standards. God sees things from a completely different perspective.

Go Climb a Tree

When Zaccheaus realized how desperately he needed Jesus, he was willing to do anything—including climbing a tree—to get to him. He dropped his pride. He dropped his politeness and was willing to look like a fool just to get close to Jesus. What obstacles do you need to rise above to get a clearer view of Jesus? Like the crowd, there can be many people, things, or ideas that block our view of God. Is your pride getting in the way? Are your puny expectations getting in the way? Is your inaccurate view of God getting in the way? It takes resourcefulness, effort and energy to find a solution like Zaccheaus did. It also means looking a little foolish according to the world's standards.

> What obstacles do you need to rise above to get a clearer view of Jesus?

This little man with a big heart touched the heart of God. Jesus noticed him immediately and wanted to grab supper with Zaccheaus. In that culture it was a huge sign of acceptance. God is honored and delighted by demonstrations of urgent, rude faith that will do whatever it takes to connect. What are you doing to show God how much you want to connect with him in a life-changing way? Go climb a tree!

Do It Quickly

Like Bartimaeus, Zacchaeus didn't waste any time responding to Jesus' call on his life. We miss out on more blessings than we can possibly imagine because we don't seize the opportunities Jesus give us. We let fear, pride and laziness stand in the way. Zacchaeus could have easily stayed up the tree. He could have said, "Well, give me a while to think it over, Jesus."

Way too many of us stay stranded out on tree limbs because we don't want to come back down and take new steps for Jesus. Sure, it's easy to get excited and charge up the tree. But when Jesus really calls and we are faced with the reality of all that means, we sometimes hesitate to jump back down with both feet into the new reality. Learn how to get down from trees as quickly as you get up them. Jesus has an exciting future planned for you!

Jesus Wants to Come Home

Have you invited Jesus to come to your house? I have met more than a few believers in Jesus who have not yet let Jesus into their homes. In other words, people accept Jesus as Lord and Savior but they try to keep him in a little God-box. They take him out of the box at church, but they put him right back in the box when they leave the doors of the church (this is clear by some people's behavior in the church parking lot on the way out!). You can't compartmentalize your relationship with God. When you truly connect with Jesus it affects your home, your work, your school, and everywhere

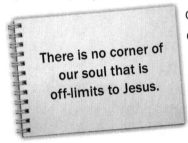

There is no corner of our soul that is off-limits to Jesus.

you go. Jesus is Lord over every aspect of our lives. There is no corner of our soul that is off-limits to Jesus. So, invite him home and watch what he can do with all your life when you surrender it all to him.

What Will Change?

When Zacchaeus claimed Jesus as Lord, he did it in the context of a radical life change. He knew his actions must match his words. Zacchaeus was not content to give Jesus mere lip service. He immediately surrendered that most precious of all commodities, his wallet! He blessed the poor and made amends to everyone he had cheated of their hard earned money. He was a changed man on the inside, and he couldn't help but show it on the outside.

I have to admit I'm a bit skeptical of people who seem to so quickly call Jesus Lord and Savior without understanding the consequences. Jesus was very clear that our faith and our actions must be in sync. When you get close to Jesus for real, it will trigger life change. You need to ask yourself how much people recognize any substantive life change in you. Our relationship with Jesus should be marked with clear evidence of faith that results in actions—large and small.

> *Fool! When will you ever learn that*
> *faith that does not result in good*
> *deeds is useless?*
>
> James 2:20

4.

DIG A HOLE

When Jesus returned to Capernaum
several days later, the news spread
quickly that he was back home. Soon
the house where he was staying was
so packed with visitors that there was
no more room, even outside the door.
While he was preaching God's word
to them, four men arrived carrying a
paralyzed man on a mat. They couldn't
bring him to Jesus because of the
crowd, so they dug a hole through
the roof above his head. Then they
lowered the man on his mat, right
down in front of Jesus. Seeing their
faith, Jesus said to the paralyzed man,
"My child, your sins are forgiven."
But some of the teachers of religious
law who were sitting there thought to
themselves, "What is he saying? This is
blasphemy! Only God can forgive sins!"
Jesus knew immediately what they
were thinking, so he asked them, "Why
do you question this in your hearts? Is
it easier to say to the paralyzed man
'Your sins are forgiven,' or 'Stand up,

*pick up your mat, and walk'? So I will
prove to you that the Son of Man has
the authority on earth to forgive sins."
Then Jesus turned to the paralyzed
man and said, "Stand up, pick up
your mat, and go home!" And the
man jumped up, grabbed his mat,
and walked out through the stunned
onlookers. They were all amazed and
praised God, exclaiming, "We've never
seen anything like this before!"*

Mark 2:1–12

Paralyzed people today face uphill battles. But at least they face these battles with motorized wheelchairs, wheelchair ramps, prosthetic devices and other accommodations increasingly available because of the American's with Disabilities Act passed by Congress. Hope is kindled in new research efforts and other medical breakthroughs. And in today's culture there is a growing sense of understanding and support for the disabled.

For first-century Capernaum, however, life was brutally difficult for a paralyzed person. There were no devices to make life a little more manageable. It would have been unimaginable for any governmental agency to pass legislation recognizing their plight and assisting them. There was no research and no hope for medical breakthroughs. And forget any understanding and support. In fact, most ancient persons shunned the paralyzed because it was widely regarded that their condition was a divine punishment for sin in their life or in the lives of their parents.

Many paralyzed persons lived as beggars, relying on the pity of their fellow townspeople for survival. It was a very isolating and depressing life that caused an utter sense of hopelessness and despair.

The paralyzed man in Mark's story was no different. He would have faced these crushing conditions and despaired over his murky future. But there was one remarkable feature about this man that set him apart from other first-century paralytics. He had friends! And these were no ordinary friends. These were the kind of friends who stick by you no matter what—friends who never stop believing in you even when you've given up on yourself. These were the kind of friends that would go the extra mile for you regardless of the time or effort involved.

And these friends knew something that would change the life of their paralyzed companion. They knew Jesus was in town! Jesus had been traveling throughout Galilee on what might be called a preaching and healing tour. He had cast out demons, healed hordes of sick people and even removed leprosy from a man. These friends, along with the rest of Capernaum, had heard these stories and even witnessed some of them for themselves.

They just knew Jesus could do something for their friend. So they scooped him up on his mat and carted him over to the house where Jesus was teaching. But apparently everyone else had the same idea. Apparently a lot of people followed Jesus' Twitter feed. The place was packed, standing room only. They couldn't even see through the front door, let alone get in to Jesus. No one was budging. Jesus was the hottest ticket in town and they were not about to give up their prime spot.

These friends could have easily looked at their paralyzed friend and said, "Sorry pal, looks like we're not seeing Jesus today. Maybe we'll try tomorrow. Hang in there." No one would have blamed them, especially not their friend. They had already done more than anybody else.

But these stubborn, thick-headed friends wouldn't give up that easily. They surveyed the situation, compared notes, brainstormed and came up with a pretty harebrained solution. Mark doesn't tell us which of the four friends came up with this "brilliant" idea. Can you imagine what it sounded like? "Hey, I know what! Let's all climb up on the roof and carry him up there on his mat. Then we'll listen for where we think Jesus is and start digging up the clay roof until we've dug a whole big enough to lower him down, right in front of Jesus! There's no way Jesus could ignore us. Sure, he's preaching and all, and it's pretty rude, but I don't care. Our friend needs help and Jesus is his best shot."

No one seemed to think they should consult with the homeowner (would the homeowner's insurance label this an "act of God?"). They also didn't seem to take into account how offended Jesus might be for this uninvited intrusion during his sermon. I know when I'm preaching in my church I don't want anyone messing with my message like that! It also didn't matter that everyone under the roof, including Jesus, was going to get pretty dusty and dirty as clods of dirt and debris came raining down on their heads during the dig!

As crazy as it sounded, there didn't seem to be any argument or disagreement, so they began executing their plan. It took time and effort, but these guys were pumped. They were on a mission and no one could stop them. They were looking for a Jesus encounter, and couldn't be deterred.

This impolite, rude and even obnoxious display of stubbornness received a smile from Jesus.

Amazingly enough, when they finally got the hole dug and their friend lowered, Jesus didn't reprimand them. He rewarded them! This impolite, rude and even obnoxious display of stubbornness received a smile from Jesus. Mark doesn't tell us what the homeowner thought about it all.

Jesus, upon seeing the unstoppable and unshakeable faith of these friends, immediately pronounced a forgiveness of sins for this paralyzed man—something which would have been inextricably tied to his healing in the mind of these Jewish onlookers. But here, just like the stories we've already seen, some of the crowd were not all that thrilled with this miraculous event unfolding before their very eyes. Jesus, however, seized this moment as an opportunity to teach about his identity and demonstrate God's glory in this healing.

Jesus looked straight at the paralytic and said, *"Stand up, take up your mat, and go home, because you are healed!"* And to everyone's astonishment, the paralyzed man did just that! And he didn't just stand up. He jumped up! Giddy with excitement, he pushed his way through the stunned onlookers who were busy exclaiming, *"We've never seen anything like this before!"*

Once he got outside he must have looked up on the roof to his thrilled friends and said, "What are you staring at? Come on down guys. Let's go home! We're going to party like never before!"

What Role Do You Play in the Story?

This story has different characters that we can identify with at various points in our life. Sometimes you may be just part of the crowd of curious onlookers, not really getting involved in the work of God happening right in front of you. You may even be skeptical or critical, like the religious teachers, always having something to complain about or question. At other times you may play the role of the homeowner, being inconvenienced because a great work of God is taking place in your otherwise "orderly" life.

But the real action takes place in the two key roles played out in this dramatic event—the paralytic and his friends. Sometimes you and I play the role of the paralytic. While we may not be physically paralyzed, we often get "disabled" in other ways. You may go through many forms of paralysis in the course of your life: financial paralysis, emotional paralysis, relational paralysis, addictive paralysis, spiritual paralysis. There are times in our lives when we feel knocked down, disoriented or totally desperate, wondering what our future holds.

These are the times when you need friends like those of the paralytic of Capernaum. You need friends who can take you to Jesus. You need friends who will do anything to get you on the right path. You need friends who will shake things up to get you close to God.

You may say, "I'm not paralyzed in any way. I'm doing fine right now." Well then, it's time for you to be a friend. That's right. More often than not, you and I have the opportunity to play the role of friend in the lives of hurting, broken and paralyzed people around us. Can you identify anyone in your life that needs help? There are people all around you who need Jesus and the healing that he alone can provide. What are you doing to bring people to Jesus?

Start Digging!

You've got to love the friends in this story. They hoped against hope, believed in the face of doubt, and made a way where there seemed to be no way. They were willing to make an effort that others wrote off as a foolish waste of time. They were willing to befriend a man that most would have given up on long ago. They were willing to think outside the box when it came to getting the attention of Jesus, even if it came across as rather brash and unconventional. And most of all, they possessed an inextinguishable faith in the power of Jesus to do something miraculous.

It was this faith that propelled them through those moments outside the house when they could have simply turned around and gone home. But their faith drove them to do whatever it took to get face-to-face with Jesus. This is the kind of faith that touched Jesus' heart and set off a chain of events that led to a remarkably changed life that day.

How does your faith compare to these friends' faith? Remember, Jesus loves to see a persistent brand of faith that rises above all obstacles and clears all hurdles. He's looking to reward a faith that hopes against all hope and makes a way where there seems to be no way. He's looking for people who are willing to get a little dirty. He's looking for people who are willing to roll up their sleeves and dig in. Start digging!

He's looking for people who are willing to get a little dirty.

Don't Listen to the Critics

This is a recurrent theme throughout these remarkable stories of faith in the gospels. Just remember, in the face of their critics, Bartimaeus wouldn't stop shouting, Zacchaeus wouldn't stop climbing, and these friends wouldn't stop digging. There will always be people who will urge you to give up and throw in the towel. There will always be people whose doubts seem to be bigger than your belief. There will always be people who will tell you it's not worth it. Don't believe them. Believe Jesus.

Jump up!

When Jesus told this paralyzed man to "Stand up," he didn't do it. Merely standing up wasn't good enough for this man. He jumped up! I have to believe at that moment Jesus must have busted out in joyous laughter. How pleased he must have been with this man's exuberant, even irreverent reaction to his newfound freedom. This reminds me as well of Bartimaeus and Zacchaues. Bartimaeus threw off his cloak to come quickly to Jesus. Zacchaeus heeded Jesus' command to come quickly scampering down the tree to embrace his new life. And here, the formerly paralyzed man jumped into his new life.

> Your impolite faith should be infectious to all the curious onlookers that surround your life—family, neighbors, friends, co-workers.

When Jesus moves in a powerful way in your life, don't resist the urge to jump up and embrace what he has done. It's not just for you. Your impolite faith should be infectious to all the curious onlookers that surround your life—family, neighbors, friends, co-workers. When the healed man jumped up and pushed his way through the crowd they all praised God at that moment and many believers were created that day. Let your exuberant faith be seen. Let your story be known. Share Jesus and what he has done in your life.

What this world needs are more people who look at the lives of bold believers and say, *"We've never seen anything like this before!"*

5.

SCREAM IN THE STORM

As evening came, Jesus said to his disciples, "Let's cross to the other side of the lake." So they took Jesus in the boat and started out, leaving the crowds behind (although other boats followed). But soon a fierce storm came up. High waves were breaking into the boat, and it began to fill with water. Jesus was sleeping at the back of the boat with his head on a cushion. The disciples woke him up, shouting, "Teacher, don't you care that we're going to drown?" When Jesus woke up, he rebuked the wind and said to the water, "Silence! Be still!"

Suddenly the wind stopped, and there was a great calm. Then he asked them, "Why are you afraid? Do you still have no faith?" The disciples were absolutely terrified. "Who is this man?" they asked each other. "Even the wind and waves obey him!"

Mark 4:35–41

It started out like any other trip across the lake. In fact, they were likely glad to be getting away from the swarming crowd. The crowd could really be suffocating sometimes. But things quickly went from good, to bad, to worse. The Sea of Galilee was 680 feet below sea level, surrounded by hilly terrain. Winds in the area around the water could quickly intensify, sometimes evoking surprise storms of great strength.

Many of the disciples were veteran fisherman and had navigated these waters for years. They had been through storms before, but this one was fierce and the water filled the boat faster than they could bail. These "pros" panicked! They just knew they were going down; and to make matters worse, Jesus was asleep in the stern of the boat.

Asleep? How could he sleep in the middle of a storm? The disciples were furious with him. They couldn't believe their master was so out of touch and unconcerned with their condition. So what do they do? They frantically woke him up, screaming in his face, *"Teacher, don't you even care that we are going to drown?"* They didn't really care about respect at this moment. Normally it is impolite and rude to wake someone from a nap—especially by screaming at the top of their lungs—but they were about to die! What other choice did they have?

I would not be a very happy camper if someone screamed in my ear while I was taking a nap! Instead of screaming at the disciples, however, Jesus screamed at the storm. His voice commanded the winds and the waves to die down. Serenity swept across the lake and across the formerly frantic hearts of the disciples.

The disciples stood in their flooded boat, staring at the calm. They looked pretty silly with water up to their knees, mouths gaping wide open at the miracle they had just witnessed. In that moment of vulnerability Jesus challenged them about their fears, wondering why they didn't trust him. He basically called them cowards and prodded them to take their faith to the next level. They could scarcely take it all in and started to talk among themselves about this amazing Rabbi who possessed such power.

Don't Be Surprised By Storms

Some Christ-followers actually believe they are immune from storms in their lives. They think if they just have enough faith, pray enough, or read the Bible enough, they won't be affected by life's stormy weather. What Bible are they reading?

It is interesting to note the disciples were engulfed by this storm while they were in the very presence of Jesus! Just being close to Jesus does not exempt us from experiencing all that life can throw at us. Jesus doesn't give us a free pass from life's inevitable squalls. Sure, following Jesus means you should avoid some self-inflicted, stupid storms. But life storms are still going to hit. If you aren't in a storm now, you've probably just come out of one or, guess what? You're about to enter one! That's life.

> If you aren't in a storm now, you've probably just come out of one or, guess what? You're about to enter one! That's life.

Even if we are in the very center of God's will, we will encounter rough weather. In fact, being in the center of God's will is the reason for some of the storms we face. Standing strong in the faith has not always been popular in any culture since the first century. The Apostle Paul was in greater alignment with God's will for his life than anyone in Christian history. But he was still beaten, imprisoned, left for dead, shipwrecked, snake-bitten, mocked and ridiculed. He was no stranger to storms.

David acknowledged this in the twenty-third psalm when he wrote: *"Even though I walk through the valley of the shadow of death..."* (Psalm 23:4 NIV). Notice David didn't write, "Thank you God, that I get to avoid all the valleys of the shadow of death!" David knew better. He had seen more than his fair share of storms and he had one of the closest relationships with the Lord in the Old Testament.

Being a Christian doesn't mean you get out of storms. It means you aren't alone in the storms. The disciples panicked because they forgot God was in the back of the boat! The very creator of wind and water was right there with them. The God who parted the waters for Moses was a few feet away. If they only knew the power in their midst, they might have been relaxed enough to catch a nap too!

> Being a Christian doesn't mean you get out of storms. It means you aren't alone in the storms.

When you have accepted Jesus Christ as your Lord and Savior he promises to dwell with you always, through the Holy Spirit. He will always be in your boat. At the end of his ministry he reminded the disciples of this when he promised them the abiding presence of the Holy Spirit: *"...I will ask the Father, and he will give you another Advocate, who will never leave you. He is the Holy Spirit..."* (John 14:16,17).

Does God Care?

The disciples accused Jesus of not caring. They felt he was disconnected from their concerns and they couldn't understand why he was asleep at the switch. They were knee deep in storm water, about to go down, and Jesus had checked out.

Do you ever feel that way? Sure you do! We've all experienced those feelings at times. We wonder why things are happening to us and why God doesn't seem to care. Why doesn't he just step in and fix it all? Now!

> Storms are temporary, but Jesus is for eternity.

We need to understand two things about storms. First, storms are temporary, but Jesus is for eternity.

> *That is why we never give up. Though our bodies are dying, our spirits are being renewed every day. For our present troubles are quite small and won't last very long. Yet they produce for us immeasurably great glory that will last forever! So we don't look at the troubles we can see right now; rather, we look forward to what we have not yet seen. For the troubles we see will soon be over, but the joys to come will last forever.*
>
> 2 Corinthians 4:16–18

Our storms pale in comparison to what lies ahead. Their temporary nature serves to highlight the permanent, enduring and eternal freedom from storms we will experience on the other side of heaven.

For Paul, storms presented an opportunity to focus on what was to come, rather than what he had to endure for a while.

Second, storms give us an opportunity to grow in Christ-likeness. They not only help us focus on heaven, but they help us bring a bit of heaven to earth. James helps us understand this concept.

> *Dear brothers and sisters, whenever trouble comes your way, let it be an opportunity for joy. For when your faith is tested, your endurance has a chance to grow. So, let it grow, for when your endurance is fully developed, you will be strong in character and ready for anything."*
> James 1:2-4

Great endurance athletes relate to this verse. They realize that hitting a rough spot in their training routine makes them push even harder. It prepares their minds and bodies for greater perseverance in the race. That's what storms are. They are merely tests. They are simply opportunities to get in better shape for the race.

I want to be described that way when people see me. "Hey, there goes Matthew Hartsfield, strong in character and ready for anything!" Sounds kind of like a super action figure. But seriously, isn't that what you want for your life—strength of character and the ability to face anything?

> God does care, but he cares more about your character than your comfort.

God does care, but he cares more about your character than your comfort. He cares more about your holiness than your happiness. God is working on you and developing you to be *"strong in character and ready for anything."* If he came and bailed us out every time we hit a rough patch we wouldn't grow at all.

I care about my two daughters. I don't want them to face any storms; but I know they will. So, I have had to learn the fine art of stepping back sometimes and letting the storms hit so they learn how to develop that strength of character. If I know how to do that—imperfectly—for my daughters, just think about how God does it perfectly with us.

Go Ahead and Scream

The disciples were literally screaming at Jesus! Their frustration level had reached the top and they let it all out. How can you blame them? They were in the middle of a storm, confused, and going down. It is natural to scream in the middle of storms.

And to make it even worse, they screamed at Jesus while he was sleeping. Have you ever been awakened to the screams of twelve wet, cold, scared guys?! I shudder at the thought. If it had been me, I might have called down lightning from heaven and taught them all a lesson they would never forget. It's a good thing I'm not God.

When Jesus wakes up he doesn't yell at the disciples for yelling at him; rather, he yells at the storm. I've always been intrigued by this. Jesus totally understood why they were screaming at him and he didn't punish them for it. They were impolitely and rudely screaming at him and accusing him of not caring, and he took it all in stride. He knew they were scared. He knew they had little faith. He knew they were confused and tired.

Jesus knows those same things about us. He understands us completely and he still loves us! At least the disciples trusted Jesus enough to come running to the back of the boat and shout. In the middle of the storm the only thing they knew to do was come running to Jesus, screaming at the top of their lungs.

When all else fails and we run out of options, do we at least have enough sense to go running to Jesus?

What a great lesson for us. When all else fails and we run out of options, do we at least have enough sense to go running to Jesus? And do we feel comfortable enough with Jesus to come screaming in the midst of our desperation? The disciples didn't have to dress up their language for Jesus and neither do you. They simply cried out from their hearts and gave Jesus everything they had. They didn't worry about how it might come across or how rude it may sound. They just knew that Jesus was the only one who could do anything about their storm and they were willing to show him their desperation.

Obviously I don't mean that we literally have to scream and shout at Jesus for him to hear us or for our prayers to be genuine and authentic. A shout from the heart in prayer simply means that we are real with Jesus, fervent in our prayers and urgent in our requests. We don't take time to dress up our prayers; rather, we let them pour unrehearsed from our hearts to the ears of our God.

Give all your worries and cares to
God, for he cares about you.
1 Peter 5:7

6.

START BEGGING

On the other side of the lake the crowds welcomed Jesus, because they had been waiting for him. Then a man named Jairus, a leader of the local synagogue, came and fell at Jesus' feet, pleading with him to come home with him. His only daughter, who was twelve years old, was dying. As Jesus went with him, he was surrounded by the crowds. A woman in the crowd had suffered for twelve years with constant bleeding, and she could find no cure. Coming up behind Jesus, she touched the fringe of his robe. Immediately, the bleeding stopped. "Who touched me?" Jesus asked. Everyone denied it, and Peter said, "Master, this whole crowd is pressing up against you." But Jesus said, "Someone deliberately touched me, for I felt healing power go out from me." When the woman realized that she could not stay hidden, she began to tremble and fell to her knees before him. The whole crowd heard her explain why she had touched him and that she had been immediately healed. "Daughter," he said to her, "your faith has made you well. Go in peace." While he was still speaking to her, a messenger arrived from the home of Jairus, the leader of the synagogue. He told him, "Your daughter is dead. There's no use troubling the Teacher now." But when Jesus heard what had happened, he said to Jairus, "Don't be afraid. Just have faith, and she will be healed." When they arrived at the house, Jesus wouldn't let anyone go in with him except Peter, John, James, and the little girl's father and mother. The house was filled with people weeping and wailing, but he said, "Stop the weeping! She isn't dead; she's only asleep." But the crowd laughed at him because they all knew she had died. Then Jesus took her by the hand and said in a loud voice, "My child, get up!" And at that moment her life returned, and she immediately stood up! Then Jesus told them to give her something to eat. Her parents were overwhelmed, but Jesus insisted that they not tell anyone what had happened.

Luke 8:40–56

Once again the crowds surrounded Jesus and his disciples. Men, women, boys and girls, they all created quite a scene wherever Jesus traveled. In the midst of these crowds there was usually a small contingent of religious officials: Pharisees, Sadducees, scribes, etc. Their primary purpose was to keep tabs on Jesus. They would sometimes ask him difficult questions, trying to make him look bad in front of all his followers. Obviously this never worked, much to the frustration of the religious leaders. These officials would hound Jesus for the duration of his earthly ministry (Matthew 22:18).

But today was different. Today a religious leader was in the crowd for personal reasons. He wasn't there to give Jesus a hard time. He came to humble himself before Jesus and seek his help. Jairus was the leader of the local synagogue, the center of religious life and worship for the community. Jairus would have been in charge of running the place and administering its affairs, supervising the worship practices. He was basically the boss. Jairus commanded a great deal of respect, holding a position of honor and prestige far beyond most of the persons in the crowd that day.

Like other religious leaders, Jairus was supposed to hold Jesus at arm's length, casting a suspicious eye on his every move. So, it caused quite a stir in the crowd when Jairus fell down at Jesus' feet begging him to come help his twelve-year-old daughter. Jairus laid his pride aside and took the posture of a submissive

> When he fell at Jesus' feet he wasn't the leader of the local synagogue, he was simply a desperate Dad at the end of his rope, willing to do anything for his dying little girl.

beggar. He didn't care about respect anymore. He didn't care about position and prestige. When he fell at Jesus' feet he wasn't the leader of the local synagogue, he was simply a desperate Dad at the end of his rope, willing to do anything for his dying little girl.

Jesus was moved by this display of faith, a faith that sought him out despite the obvious embarrassment for Jairus. Jesus knew what it took for Jairus to swallow his pride. He was also aware of the prestige that Jairus might be forfeiting among his colleagues and the rest of the community. So, Jesus began the walk to Jairus' house right away.

On the way, another story unfolded in the crowd. A woman, like Jairus, was also in desperate need that day. She, too, was on a mission to get close to Jesus. But we will wait for the next chapter to explore her story in more detail. Suffice it to say, however, that because Jesus stopped to minister to this woman it caused a delay during which Jairus' daughter died.

Messengers from Jairus' house came running with the bad news and told them stop bothering Jesus: *"There's no use troubling the Teacher now."* In that moment a flood of emotions and questions must have come to Jairus' mind. "Why couldn't they have walked more swiftly?" "Why was the crowd getting in the way?" "Who is this woman to think she can get her healing at the expense of my daughter's healing?"

But Jesus immediately intervened and said some of the most reassuring words in all of Scripture: *"Don't be afraid. Just trust me and she'll be all right"* (TLB). Jairus felt strangely calmed by these words and they pressed on, staring death in the face, hoping against hope.

When Jesus and the procession finally arrived at the house they were met by the family, friends and mourners who were already creating quite a racket with their weeping and wailing. Jesus entered the house with Jairus, Jairus' wife, and his inner circle of disciples, Peter, James and John. Jesus looked at the mourners and offered no words of sympathy. Instead he told them to be quiet; the little girl was only sleeping.

Immediately the mourning turned to laughter, but not happy laughter. This was mocking laughter that ridiculed Jesus. These people knew that girl was dead and they couldn't believe Jesus was trying to tell them otherwise. But Jesus ignored them and went straight to the girl, took her hand and commanded her in a loud voice to get up! Immediately her life returned and he ordered her parents to give her something to eat so no one could claim she was just a ghost of some sort. Jairus, his wife and all the household were left overwhelmed and speechless.

Push Beyond the Pride

Jairus had a lot to lose that day. Approaching Jesus the way he did was unheard of for religious leaders. We will see in another chapter that Nicodemus, a Pharisee, approached Jesus only under the cover of night. Jairus could lose his respect. He could lose his prestige. He could even lose his job. But all Jairus could think about losing was his daughter.

I can certainly understand how Jairus must have felt, being the father of two daughters myself. Like me, Jairus would go to any lengths to get help for his little girl. Jairus knew Jesus was a healer like none other. Jairus knew he was from God. Jairus knew Jesus had just arrived in town and he didn't want to miss his chance at getting close to Jesus.

> Many of us miss our opportunity to get close to Jesus because we let our pride get in the way.

Many of us miss our opportunity to get close to Jesus because we let our pride get in the way. We think we're in control. We think we can run our lives just fine without any input from God. We don't want to appear desperate or needy in any way. We don't want people to think we don't have our act together. And we especially don't want to humble ourselves and beg!

The most valuable lesson we learn from Jairus' is how to be humble. The humility of Jairus immediately captivated Jesus' heart and he wanted to go straight to his house. God has always honored humility and disdained pride. In fact, pride shuts the door on God's miracles with a loud slam!

> *Pride first, then the crash,*
> *but humility is precursor to honor.*
> Proverbs 18:12 (MSG)

Go Ahead, Bother Jesus!

When the messengers came to tell Jairus that his daughter had died they said something interesting, *"There's no use troubling the Teacher now."* Jesus had just returned from the other side of the lake and Jairus immediately seized him and begged him to come to his house. Everyone knew that Jairus had asked Jesus to go out of his way. In reality he was "troubling" the Teacher.

But we must understand that Jesus loves to be "bothered" by us. He wants you to approach him with that seemingly contradictory blend of boldness and humility (sometimes it looks pretty

But we must understand that Jesus loves to be "bothered" by us.

rude!). He loved to see the boldness and humbleness in Jairus and would have gone to the ends of the earth to minister to a heart like that!

When you have accepted Jesus as your Lord and Savior you are adopted as a son or daughter into God's family. Your heavenly Father wants you to "bother" him and seek his help. When my two girls need my help I don't want them to hesitate to ask me. I may look busy. I may seem distracted, but whatever it takes, I hope they grab my attention and tell me what's on their heart. I can still remember when they were little and sometimes had to place both hands on my cheeks and turn my head toward them! God is waiting for you to bother him that way. What are you waiting for?

A Powerful Promise

At Jairus' lowest moment, when he thought his daughter was dead, Jesus knew exactly what he needed to hear. Jesus uttered the words that you and I desperately need to hear as well, *"Don't be afraid. Just trust me and she'll be all right"* (TLB). Those words become a powerful promise when you actually trust Jesus, believe in him and give your life to him. Where do you need to hear those words spoken to you at this moment? Think about it. Right now, as you are reading these pages, where do you need Jesus to show up in a powerful way and say to you, *"Don't be afraid. Just trust me and she'll be all right"* (TLB).

Jesus said similar words to his disciples the last night he spent with them on earth. In the upper room, during the last supper, the disciples were confused, scared and uncertain about the future. It was a pretty dark and slippery moment in their life when Jesus looked straight at them and said: *"Don't let your hearts be troubled. Trust in God, and trust also in me. I am leaving you with a gift—peace of mind and heart. And the peace I give is a gift the world cannot give. So don't be troubled or afraid"* (John 14:1,27).

Go ahead; accept this precious gift of peace. Accept Jesus. Seek him out. Fall down before him. Drop your pride. "Bother" him. Invite him to come to your house to heal whatever needs healing. Like Jairus, your life will never be the same again.

7.

CLAW THROUGH CROWDS

*On the other side of the lake the
crowds welcomed Jesus, because they
had been waiting for him. Then a man
named Jairus, a leader of the local
synagogue, came and fell at Jesus'
feet, pleading with him to come home
with him. His only daughter, who was
twelve years old, was dying. As Jesus
went with him, he was surrounded by
the crowds. A woman in the crowd had
suffered for twelve years with constant
bleeding, and she could find no cure.
Coming up behind Jesus, she touched
the fringe of his robe. Immediately, the
bleeding stopped. "Who touched me?"
Jesus asked. Everyone denied it, and
Peter said, "Master, this whole crowd
is pressing up against you." But Jesus
said, "Someone deliberately touched
me, for I felt healing power go out
from me." When the woman realized
that she could not stay hidden, she
began to tremble and fell to her knees
before him. The whole crowd heard her
explain why she had touched him and*

*that she had been immediately healed.
"Daughter," he said to her, "your faith
has made you well. Go in peace."
While he was still speaking to her, a
messenger arrived from the home of
Jairus, the leader of the synagogue.
He told him, "Your daughter is dead.
There's no use troubling the Teacher
now." But when Jesus heard what had
happened, he said to Jairus, "Don't
be afraid. Just have faith, and she will
be healed." When they arrived at the
house, Jesus wouldn't let anyone go
in with him except Peter, John, James,
and the little girl's father and mother.
The house was filled with people
weeping and wailing, but he said,
"Stop the weeping! She isn't dead;
she's only asleep." But the crowd
laughed at him because they all knew
she had died. Then Jesus took her by
the hand and said in a loud voice, "My
child, get up!" And at that moment
her life returned, and she immediately
stood up! Then Jesus told them to give
her something to eat. Her parents
were overwhelmed, but Jesus insisted
that they not tell anyone
what had happened.*

Luke 8:40–56

Here's the story inside a story. In the previous chapter we saw how Jairus came to Jesus, desperate for his daughter to be healed. As they were making their way to Jairus' house, a woman worked her way into the crowd surrounding Jesus. It would not have been unusual for women to be part of that mob scene following Jesus. This woman, however, had no business being there.

She was sick, very sick. She was in a desperately weakened condition having hemorrhaged for over twelve years! She had tried everything, spending a fortune on doctors only to find no cure, no hope. Her life was wasting away on a daily basis and there was no way to stem the tide.

And to make matters worse, her physical condition was not her only problem. According to Jewish law, any menstruating woman (whether by natural cycle or illness) was ceremonially "unclean." Also, any man touching a menstruating woman would be declared "unclean," and would have to go through a prescribed purification process (Leviticus 15:19 and 20:18). So, the past twelve years had been marked by physical weakness and social isolation. Her future was bleak. Each day was marked by more weakness, more pain, and more isolation.

But not today! Jesus was in town. Just the thought of Jesus lifted her spirits and ignited her courage. She had heard the stories about this itinerant Rabbi and a flicker of hope began to course through her veins. Maybe Jesus could do something about her condition, but was it worth fighting the crowd? Was it worth the risk of getting noticed in the crowd in an "unclean" state? Was it worth expending the precious little energy she had that day? Yes! It was all worth it. She knew he had changed other people's lives and she was ready for a change. She was well aware of his miraculous healings and she believed he could heal her as well.

> For the first time in years she allowed herself to hope!

She was a believer! For the first time in years she allowed herself to hope!

This was not going to be easy. The crowd was thick and it was moving quickly toward Jairus' house. She had to keep up. She had to make her way, clawing through the crowd in her weakened condition. And she had to do it as quietly as possible. She was on a clandestine mission. She couldn't be noticed and she certainly didn't want to stop the procession. She didn't want to draw Jesus' attention or even let him know she had touched him. She was unclean. She shouldn't be touching any man, let alone a Rabbi! She thought to herself, "If only I can get to the fringe of his robe and touch it I will be healed. I'll get in and get out. No one will notice."

With every ounce of strength she could muster she finally got within arm's length of Jesus. She was in striking distance and the excitement was making her head spin. With a quick brush of her hand she touched his robe. Immediately she felt strength return to her body. It was like a rush of refreshing energy and it must have been a surprise to her how quickly it all took place. She hadn't felt like this in twelve years, and she didn't need any doctors to confirm what she knew deep inside. "I'm finally free!"

But that's when things got messy. To her horror Jesus stopped! Her mind began racing, "Did he notice? How could he, I barely touched his robe?" She remained frozen, trying to blend into the crowd to see what would happen. Her knees began to weaken even though she had new strength. "What will Jesus do to me?"

Jesus asked a curious question. *"Who touched me?"* The disciples, Jairus, and everyone else looked strangely at Jesus, thinking maybe he had been out in the sun too long. *"What do you mean?"* they asked, *"Everyone's bumping up next to you! We've all touched you because it's so crowded and crazy in this mob."*

Obviously Jesus knew who had touched him, but he stopped to make this a teaching moment for the woman and everyone in the crowd that day. He wanted to make sure she didn't have any "magical" notions about the fringe of his garment. He wanted her and crowd to know in no uncertain terms that she had touched the very heart of God and that her healing was directly from him. In the midst of their confusion Jesus reiterated, *"No, someone deliberately touched me, for I felt healing power go out from me."* Amazing! Jesus was actually physically affected when he healed someone. He actually felt a discharge of power, as if he were giving away something of himself to every person he healed.

Well this was it. The woman knew she couldn't hide it any longer. She had to face the music. She had to confess. Falling to her knees with fear and trembling, she told the story to Jesus and the crowd. She was ready for her rebuke and her punishment. She began to wonder if she had made the right decision. "What was I thinking?"

As she sat there on her knees, shaking and trembling, Jesus uttered a word that would forever change her heart the way her body had been changed. It was a word that would change the way she, and the crowd, would think about God. Jesus said, "Daughter." Daughter! It was a term of endearment, not rebuke. He didn't say "Woman!" or "How dare you!" or "Stone her!" He said, "Daughter," and it made all the difference in the world. She realized at that moment that she was on her knees worshipping an approachable God who cared more about her than religious laws and societal protocol.

And Jesus continued: *"...your faith has made you well, Go in peace."* Jesus recognized the faith and courage it took for her to claw her way through the crowd to get to him. He rewarded her for her boldness and her brashness. She was willing to bend the rules, even break the rules in order to get to Jesus. She was willing to risk it all and Jesus had to be amazed and thrilled by a faith like that. He commended her faith and gave her a blessing of peace as she started the first day of her brand-new life!

A Study in Contrasts

This woman was on the opposite end of the spectrum from Jairus. He held a position of respect and was highly honored in the community. She had nothing and was considered a social outcast. They were polar opposites on the socio-economic landscape and shared nothing in common. But one thing united them, their desperation to get to Jesus. Like Bartimaeus and Zacchaeus, the woman and Jairus were bound together that day by a common desperation and a common faith in Jesus as their only hope.

Once again, Jesus demonstrates that he is available to everyone and wants to be approached no matter what you feel you have or don't have going for you.

Once again, Jesus demonstrates that he is available to everyone and wants to be approached no matter what you feel you have or don't have going for you. Have you ever felt you were too good for Jesus? Or, more likely, have you ever felt you had no business getting next to Jesus? Have you ever felt "unclean?" I am constantly amazed by people who tell me they don't think they should be in church because of their lifestyle or because of events from their past they cannot shake. They don't feel like God wants to hear from them, or if he does, it's only so he can punish them.

Jesus welcomes you with open arms. He welcomes you if you are like Jairus—respected, honored, well-positioned. And he welcomes you if you are like this woman—weak, outcast, on the fringe. It just doesn't matter. Let the one thing that Jairus and the woman shared that day be the one thing that changes your life as well, a bold faith in Jesus.

Claw Through the Crowd

This woman had no strength. She was basically anemic from her years of hemorrhaging. What little strength she had, however, she was willing to expend to get to Jesus. She had faith that if she gave everything she had to pursue Jesus he would multiply her strength beyond imagination. She reminds me of the little boy who offered his five barley loaves and two fish to Jesus so that he might feed the crowd of thousands (John 6:9).

This is faith that stirs the heart of God. In order for a miracle to happen in your life, you need to be willing to pursue God with all you have, holding nothing back. God wants us to trust him for our needs and place our faith in his multiplication of blessings in our lives.

This woman was willing to fight through the crowd. Are you? Are you willing to do whatever it takes to get to Jesus? Granted, you don't have to fight through a physical crowd to get to Jesus in the form of a man from Nazareth. However, you most likely have other crowds to fight.

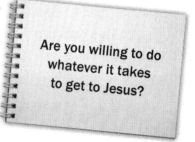

Are you willing to do whatever it takes to get to Jesus?

These are the crowds in our minds and hearts. Sometimes we have to fight through a crowd of doubt. Sometimes we face a crowd of regrets and resentments from our past that keep us tied up and locked down. Other times we face a crowd of skepticism that keeps us from fully releasing our hearts to Jesus. Sometimes we fight a crowd of pride that keeps us imprisoned in our own selves. These crowds can be worse than fighting through a physical crowd. But the fight is worth it. It was worth it for Jairus and this woman. It will be worth it to you as well. Whatever it takes, get to Jesus.

Don't Just Rub Elbows with Jesus

Peter looked at Jesus and said, *"Master, this whole crowd is pressing up against you."* But if that were the case, then why didn't everybody in the crowd receive a healing that day? Surely in a crowd that size there were people who had pains, aches, ailments and diseases. If everybody was touching Jesus, why didn't healing power discharge from him to a mass of people in the throngs that were processing to Jairus' home?

The woman was the only one in the great crowd that actually touched Jesus in faith. And that made all the difference. She was desperate to get to Jesus and she believed he was her only hope. She touched him deliberately, from the deepest place of longing in her soul. That was no casual touch.

Many people today have a passing acquaintance with Jesus. A lot of us brush up against him all the time. We go to church, sing songs, listen to sermons. Maybe we go to a class or two or a small group at church. We might even serve and give faithfully. Now all of this is uplifting and there is value in each of these routine practices. But how many of us really reach out to deliberately touch Jesus?

Are you satisfied with just bumping up against Jesus occasionally? Do you really want to spend your life just rubbing elbows with Jesus, but never feeling his power flow into your soul and body? When you approach Jesus, do you really expect great things to happen? When you approach

> When you approach Jesus, do you really expect great things to happen?

Jesus, are you content with just touching his garment, or do you want to grab him, hold him, and never let go?

Jesus wants to deliberately touch you, but you have to be willing to deliberately touch Jesus. He is looking for our earnest, sincere, fervent hearts to come to him in prayer, humbly and boldly reaching out to him as the one person in a crowded world who can make a difference in our lives. Go ahead, claw through your crowded mind and heart and grab hold of Jesus with everything you have!

8.

SNEAK THROUGH DARKNESS

There was a man named Nicodemus,
a Jewish religious leader who was a
Pharisee. After dark one evening, he
came to speak with Jesus. "Rabbi,"
he said, "we all know that God has
sent you to teach us. Your miraculous
signs are evidence that God is with
you." Jesus replied, "I tell you the truth,
unless you are born again, you cannot
see the Kingdom of God." "What do
you mean?" exclaimed Nicodemus.
"How can an old man go back into his
mother's womb and be born again?"
Jesus replied, "I assure you, no one
can enter the Kingdom of God without
being born of water and the Spirit.
Humans can reproduce only human
life, but the Holy Spirit gives birth to
spiritual life. So don't be surprised
when I say, 'You must be born again.'
The wind blows wherever it wants. Just
as you can hear the wind but can't
tell where it comes from or where it is

*going, so you can't explain how people
are born of the Spirit." "How are these
things possible?" Nicodemus asked.*

John 3:1–9

Nicodemus was like Jairus, a highly respected religious leader of the day. Nicodemus, however, was even more highly exalted than Jairus. He was a Pharisee, one of the group of people who hounded Jesus and antagonized him throughout his ministry. The Pharisees were threatened by Jesus because he undermined their authority and called their views into question on a frequent basis. And not only was Nicodemus a Pharisee, he was also a member of the Sanhedrin, the ruling council in Jerusalem that sought to bring Jesus down in disgrace.

Nicodemus was highly educated, well-connected and powerful by all worldly standards. Jesus, however, made him wonder what he was missing. When he heard Jesus teach and witnessed his miracles, he knew his education was lacking, his connections were dubious and his power was fleeting. Deep down inside he wanted real learning, real connection and real power. He knew Jesus was sent from God, but Nicodemus was confused. What did it all mean? How could he find out? Surely he couldn't approach Jesus with all his questions. Or could he?

Nicodemus was afraid of meeting with Jesus in broad daylight. He didn't want to be discovered. He wasn't quite ready to take that risk and lose everything. But rather than giving up, he decided to come to Jesus under the cover of darkness, hoping he wouldn't be noticed. It was an inconvenient time for Jesus, but Nicodemus was desperate for truth, and he knew Jesus was his only true source.

When Nicodemus got face-to-face with Jesus, he made a startling admission for a Pharisee. He acknowledged that Jesus was from God and that his miracles were definitely proof of God's involvement. He wanted desperately to believe, but he wasn't ready to take the leap. Jesus needed to do some work on his heart and he wasted no time. He challenged Nicodemus' mind and spirit like no one had ever done. He cut right to Nicodemus' core, exposing all of his inadequacies and insecurities.

In telling Nicodemus he had to be born again, he was basically saying he had to surrender everything and become a child again—a child that could be adopted into God's family. He had to admit his childlike need for God, his ignorance of deeper truths, and his

In telling Nicodemus he had to be born again, he was basically saying he had to surrender everything and become a child again—a child that could be adopted into God's family utter dependence on the unpredictable winds of the Holy Spirit. These were things that Pharisees were not accustomed to doing!

It was all mind-boggling for Nicodemus and he asked more than once, *"What do you mean?"* Nicodemus was used to having people ask him that question, not the other way around. But now Jesus was the teacher and Nicodemus was the student, a learner who was becoming acutely aware of how much he didn't know.

Before Nicodemus left that night his mind had been opened, his heart had been touched and his soul was thawing. His life was changing. Later in John's gospel we see evidence of this life change and growing faith in Jesus. He stood up to the other leaders and defended Jesus, much to his own detriment. After Jesus hung dead on the cross it was Nicodemus who joined Joseph of Arimathea in removing his body and preparing it for a proper burial. Nicodemus sacrificed a great deal to purchase the seventy-five pounds of embalming ointment of myrrh and aloes that were needed to bury a body in a respectful manner. He gave up his time, his money and his personal security to do all this for the man he loved so deeply and who he now believed was the Messiah.

Always Something to Learn

The Pharisees were among the educated elite of the Jewish culture. There were few people who could tell them anything. Most of the Pharisees let this arrogance stand in the way of what God wanted to teach them. Not Nicodemus. He was willing to come to Jesus with an open mind and an open heart, trusting him for knowledge and wisdom. He was a man with many questions and he was convinced Jesus had the answers.

You probably have a lot of questions yourself, but are you always convinced that Jesus has all the answers? Are you willing to come to Jesus as a student, a learner searching for the truth? A search for the truth is actually a search for Jesus. Jesus didn't teach one truth out of many possible options. Jesus himself was the embodiment of objective truth. To "Doubting Thomas" he said: *"I am the way, the truth and the life. No one can come to the Father except through me"* (John 14:6). Nicodemus' search for the truth was a search for God.

> A search for the truth is actually a search for Jesus.

Most of us spend our lives searching for meaning, purpose and direction for our lives. For many people this search leads them up many blind alleys and dead ends. Our culture will go to ridiculous lengths to find wisdom—flipping Tarot cards, calling psychic hotlines, reading crystals, checking our horoscope, and getting hopelessly mired in shallow human philosophies. We wonder why we end up disillusioned and frustrated. Knowing Jesus as the ultimate truth allows us to boldly seek him and expect answers from him that we can trust—answers upon which we can build our lives. James wrote: *"If you want to know what God wants you to do, ask him, and he will gladly tell you, for he is always ready to give a bountiful supply of wisdom to all who ask him; he will not resent it"* (James 1:5 TLB). That's exactly what Nicodemus did, and Jesus didn't resent it or reprimand him; rather, he taught him the deeper truths he had been searching for his whole life.

Light Up the Night

Nicodemus was in the dark not just because the sun had set on that day. Nicodemus was in the dark spiritually. He was in the dark emotionally. He was in the dark about God and God's wonderful love for him. We must recognize how much we

> If you don't know how dark it is around you, then you don't realize how much you need the light.

are in the dark before we will ever seek the light. If you don't know how dark it is around you, then you don't realize how much you need the light.

But when the bright light of Jesus shines, it presents a stark contrast to the darkness that surrounds so many of us. At the beginning of John's gospel we are told: *"Eternal life is in him, and this life gives light to all mankind. His life is the light that shines through the darkness—and the darkness can never extinguish it"* (John 1:4,5 TLB). How dark are things around you? Where is there hurt, pain or confusion that keeps you stumbling and groping? Proverbs 4:18 says: *"The way of the righteous is like the first gleam of dawn, which shines brighter until the full light of day."*

The first gleam of dawn was beginning to shine in Nicodemus' soul that fateful night. And it shined brighter and brighter as the days and weeks progressed. Once Nicodemus opened his heart to Jesus and became a truth seeker his life was forever in a state of transformation. He shone brighter and brighter at each new moment of darkness. In the midst of his hatred-spewing colleagues he stood up and defended Jesus (John 7:50-52). In the darkest moment of all, following Jesus' crucifixion, he came to retrieve the body and risk his life to show his respect for Jesus (John 19:38-42).

Make Your Move

Some might criticize Nicodemus for coming at night to see Jesus, labeling him a coward. But I believe he was one of the bravest, boldest seekers in the New Testament. He had more to lose than anybody, yet he took the first step. Sure it was a clandestine step, but he took it anyway. It was impolite to interrupt Jesus' evening, but he took the step. He could have sent some of his underlings to "check out" the teachings of Jesus and report back. No. Nicodemus had to have a personal encounter with Jesus, even if it meant inconveniencing him by coming at night. But this was no inconvenience for Jesus. Remember, it was no bother for Jesus to be "troubled" by Jairus. Whenever we are sincerely seeking truth, Jesus welcomes us at all times.

So, do whatever it takes to have a personal encounter with Jesus. Be a truth seeker. Come in the middle of the darkness that envelops our world and discover how beautiful it can be to live in the light.

9.

KEEP ON ASKING

Then Jesus left Galilee and went north to the region of Tyre. He didn't want anyone to know which house he was staying in, but he couldn't keep it a secret. Right away a woman who had heard about him came and fell at his feet. Her little girl was possessed by an evil spirit, and she begged him to cast out the demon from her daughter. Since she was a Gentile, born in Syrian Phoenicia, Jesus told her, "First I should feed the children—my own family, the Jews. It isn't right to take food from the children and throw it to the dogs." She replied, "That's true, Lord, but even the dogs under the table are allowed to eat the scraps from the children's plates." "Good answer!" he said. "Now go home, for the demon has left your daughter." And when she arrived home, she found her little girl lying quietly in bed, and the demon was gone.

Mark 7:24–30

Jesus was on the move again. This time he headed north from Galilee into the farther reaches of his travels, the area around Tyre and Sidon. In Mark's gospel we are told he and the disciples were trying to avoid the crowds, but that attempt failed miserably. As soon as he arrived in the region he was approached by a woman whose daughter was possessed by a demon. She too had heard the stories about this roaming Rabbi and was convinced he was from God and could help. Like Jairus, she was there for the sake of her daughter. Her desperation drove her to interrupt Jesus and demand that he release her daughter from this demon's control.

She immediately acknowledged her belief in Jesus, addressing him as "Lord, Son of David." Even as a Gentile she knew this was how the Messiah was to be addressed. This was an amazing display of faith and certainly Jesus and the disciples were thrilled at this encounter with a non-Jew. After all, she acknowledged his absolute control over the spiritual realm.

But Jesus did something surprising. He completely ignored her, not even saying a word. Where was his famous compassion? The disciples didn't realize that Jesus was positioning them for a teaching moment and they insisted that Jesus tell her to scram. "She's bothering us." And then, to make matters worse for this woman, Jesus told her his primary mission was for the people of Israel, not for Gentiles like herself.

The disciples must have smiled in their ignorant smugness. But to the woman, this must have come as a crushing blow. Anyone else would have silently retreated and licked their wounds. But not this woman! She wasn't deterred at all. She came right back at Jesus, fell on her knees and worshiped him, "Lord, help me!"

Jesus continued the "sparring match" and gave her a metaphor any Gentile would have understood, "It isn't right to take food from the children and throw it to the dogs." It was common for Jews to use the word "dog" as a derisive put down to the Gentile people. Ouch! Certainly she'd pick up on the hint now and throw in the towel. What was she thinking, interrupting the disciples and pressing her point so much?

But instead of turning tail and walking away, she picked up on the metaphor and turned it right back on Jesus, "Yes, Lord, but even the dogs are permitted to eat crumbs that fall beneath their master's table." Amazing, she got right back in Jesus' face and refused to take no for an answer. The disciples must have been beside themselves at the impudence of this woman. Who did she think she was, talking to Jesus like that?

> Who did she think she was, talking to Jesus like that?

This is when Jesus finally revealed that he was testing her. "Woman," he said, "your faith is great. Your request is granted." Yes! She got what she came for. Her daughter is healed. The disciples must have looked pretty sheepish when they saw Jesus turn their smugness upside down in his demonstration of love for an "outsider" to the faith.

Bothering Jesus Again!

This should be familiar territory by now. Here is another person "bothering" Jesus. The disciples are pretty pointed about how they feel about this interruption. Do you remember the critics faced by Bartimaeus, Zacchaeus and the paralytic? Do you remember the crowd the bleeding woman had to claw her way through to get to Jesus? Well now the disciples are just another part of the unsympathetic crowd. They remain unaware of a miracle that is about to unfold before their very eyes. All they can see is an "outsider" who is bothering them and taking up their time.

But let's remember something very important. You are not a bother to Jesus! Jesus loved this woman's brash faith that refused to take no for an answer. That's the whole point, isn't it? Jesus wants to reward faith that perseveres, faith that endures, faith that never gives up. More than anyone else, this woman demonstrated how to move beyond a polite faith, not settling for anything other than a direct encounter with the power of Jesus.

Keep on Asking!

I wonder how long this woman would have pestered Jesus until she got a positive response. Something tells me they would have had to drag her away kicking and screaming. She even told Jesus she would settle for crumbs! She was not leaving the table until she got something! Whether it was a five course meal or morsels that fell to the floor, she was not leaving empty handed!

How easily do you give up? How quickly do you throw in the towel? How long are you willing to persist in prayer with Jesus? If we come in sincere faith, Jesus always

> How easily do you give up? How quickly do you throw in the towel?

has something for us. It may not be exactly what we've asked for, but Jesus will never leave us empty handed. He knows what we need better than we can possibly imagine. But we need to understand what's going on with this story.

Jesus wanted to see the condition of this woman's heart. He wanted to know how much she was willing to persevere, trust and fly her faith up the flag pole no matter how much it got shot down. Prayer is not so much about the content of what we pray for as it is the context in which we pray. Jesus' heart is touched by the sincere, fervent, unflagging zeal of our prayers that will not let go. We have seen over and over that Jesus rewards faith that moves beyond politeness. He wants us to understand our desperate dependence on him. He always has something for you!

He's not toying with us or playing a cat and mouse game. No, he is building our faith. And more than that, he is building a relationship with us. He wants us to spend time with him, sharing our deepest desires, needs and dreams. If he acted like a heavenly genie and snapped his fingers over every little request, we would never spend any substantive time with him. But this woman came back again and again. Jesus wants us coming back to him again and again, building our faith, building our trust, building our relationship with him. Do you want the blessing more than the one who blesses?

I want Jesus to say to me what he said to this woman: "Matthew, your faith is great. Your request is granted." I want Jesus to be overwhelmed at my great and persevering faith. I want to keep on coming back.

Don't you? Don't you want him to say the same thing to you? "_____, your faith is great. Your request is granted." Keep asking!

Jesus Loves Outsiders

Even though he was testing this woman and his disciples, Jesus was always very clear that he came to offer himself for the whole world. Here, and in the next chapter, we'll see how much Jesus was impressed by Gentiles who came running to him with unstoppable faith. Sometimes you may feel like a spiritual outsider, like you don't have what other "super believers" have. You may watch some people and think they have a more clear line to the Father's heart than you do. Some people think my prayers as a pastor are more direct to the Father's heart than the "common" church member. I must admit, I have no hotline to God!

That's when you need to remember this story. That's when you need to remember what Jesus said to the Pharisees: *"I'm here to invite outsiders, not coddle insiders"* (Matthew 9:13b MSG). Jesus has wide open arms for you no matter how far outside you feel. Jesus' mission was to seek and save the lost, the outsiders, those who needed him most. You are

> Jesus has wide open arms for you no matter how far outside you feel.

never so far outside the family of God that you cannot be welcomed with open arms. Come to Jesus like this woman and feel like an outsider who has just come in from the cold to sit down by a warm fire.

10.

PUSH BEYOND BOUNDARIES

At that time the highly valued slave of a Roman officer was sick and near death. When the officer heard about Jesus, he sent some respected Jewish elders to ask him to come and heal his slave. So they earnestly begged Jesus to help the man. "If anyone deserves your help, he does," they said, "for he loves the Jewish people and even built a synagogue for us." So Jesus went with them. But just before they arrived at the house, the officer sent some friends to say, "Lord, don't trouble yourself by coming to my home, for I am not worthy of such an honor. I am not even worthy to come and meet you. Just say the word from where you are, and my servant will be healed. I know this because I am under the authority of my superior officers, and I have authority over my soldiers. I only need to say, 'Go,' and they go, or 'Come,' and they come. And if I say to my slaves, 'Do this,' they do it." When Jesus heard this, he was amazed.

> *Turning to the crowd that was following*
> *him, he said, "I tell you, I haven't*
> *seen faith like this in all Israel!" And*
> *when the officer's friends returned to*
> *his house, they found the slave*
> *completely healed.*
>
> Luke 7:2–10

There was no love lost between Roman soldiers and Jewish citizens. The occupying force was a daily reminder of a foreign emperor's rule and reign over their homeland. At times tensions would flare and futile attempts at revolt would break out among the more zealous Jews. For the most part, a "peaceful" co-existence marked the occupation.

But these Romans were Gentiles, non-believers in the God of Abraham, Isaac, Jacob and Joseph. They were outsiders to the faith and were thus considered "unclean" to the Jewish people (Acts 10:28). The soldiers professed loyalty to the emperor and pledged to worship him as a god. They grew up without the knowledge of the one true God the Jews worshipped. They considered the Jews odd and full of strange customs. For the most part, however, they let the Jews go about their strange festivals and religious practices. The Roman soldiers and Jews simply tried to go about their business in a benign neglect of each other.

But there was a Roman centurion in Capernaum who was different, very different. Like other centurion's, he held a position of respect and authority in the army, commanding a hundred soldiers. Unlike other centurions, however, he had a special affection for the Jewish people. He had chosen to involve himself in the local life of the Jews, building relationships with them and even constructing a synagogue for them. This was a unique demonstration of respect for the Jewish religion, and it indicated this centurion was open to seeking the truth about God, recognizing that the Jews were the chosen people of God.

So, when the centurion was in dire need, it was natural for him to turn to this famous Rabbi that had captivated the hearts of the residents of Capernaum. He had heard the stories and believed deeply that Jesus possessed power that could come only from God himself. He believed deeply that Jesus could heal his slave who had become seriously ill and was near death. He believed deeply that Jesus brought the only hope in which he could rely.

This centurion was willing to move beyond the accepted social and religious boundaries to reach out to Jesus. He, like the Gentile woman in Tyre, couldn't care less about the accepted "borders" that

> They were desperate and they knew Jesus was the only one who could come to their rescue.

were supposed to keep them from Jesus. They were desperate and they knew Jesus was the only one who could come to their rescue. Fortunately for the Roman centurion, he had been building bridges of trust with the Jewish people, and it was easier for him to seek out a Rabbi's help than it would have been for other Romans who had kept their distance from God's people.

The centurion was used to delegation and giving orders, so he sent people to tell Jesus of his dying slave. Jesus immediately responded, despite the fact he was a Roman centurion, and began to walk to his house. Before they arrived, however, something happened that elicited one of the most fantastic statements Jesus would ever utter.

The Roman centurion, because he was respectful of Jewish ways, realized that a Rabbi should not be expected to enter the home of an "unclean" Gentile. He sent another delegation to Jesus with a message—a message that deeply touched the heart of Jesus. The centurion wanted Jesus to know he was aware of authority. As a commander of troops, he knew his soldiers would obey his orders, even if he wasn't present when the orders were issued. Likewise, as a soldier himself, he reported to his superior officers and followed through on their orders without question. So he requested that Jesus conduct this healing long distance so he wouldn't have to enter an "unclean" house.

This stopped Jesus in his tracks! He immediately seized upon this as a teaching moment and addressed the ever-present crowd that was following him to the centurion's home. The centurion had, for all practical purposes, professed his faith in Christ as Messiah. He acknowledged that Jesus was the "Commander in Chief" of the spiritual realm. He was able to grasp the truth that Jesus was ultimately in control of the forces and powers that were beyond their human grasp. Jesus was God!

Jesus exclaimed, "I haven't seen faith like this in all Israel!" Jesus came for the whole world, but first and foremost he came for God's lost sheep, his chosen people, the nation of Israel. God's people were supposed to "get it" before anyone else. They were supposed to embrace the truth and profess faith in Christ before anyone else in the world.

But here a Gentile—a Roman centurion of all people—was the one to "get it." This Gentile had something to teach the nation of Israel and Jesus stopped to celebrate his faith, and at the same time, heal his slave!

Move Beyond the Boundaries

This centurion, like the woman in Tyre, paid no attention to his "place" in life. He didn't care about the boundary markers that were supposed to keep him away from Jesus. This Gentile was impolite enough to impose upon a Jewish Rabbi solely because he had faith in him. While everyone else was trying feverishly to maintain the walls that kept people apart, this centurion and Jesus were busy tearing down these walls.

Are you paying too much attention to the artificial boundary markers in your life?

Are you paying too much attention to the artificial boundary markers in your life? How willing are you to move outside your comfort zone in order to have a powerful Jesus-encounter? This centurion was willing to look foolish in order to seek help from Jesus. He was willing to have his soldiers misunderstand. He was willing to appear weak when he had spent his whole career training to be strong. He was supposed to be in command. Now, he was willing to let someone else be in charge.

It is difficult to let Jesus call the shots in our lives. But every day I must be willing to be like the Roman centurion. I must turn over those things in my life over which I think I have control. I must be willing to let Jesus be the commanding officer in my life. I have to give up the illusion that I've got it all under control, that somehow I have authority when only Jesus has true authority. The centurion gave up control and admitted he needed Jesus when he was facing a crisis. All too often you and I wait for a crisis before we'll tear down the walls and get closer to Jesus.

Don't wait! Every day we need to be tearing down the walls that keep us from Jesus—walls of pride, walls of control, walls of guilt, walls of shame, walls of hate, walls, walls, walls! Tear down the walls, move the boundaries, cross the borders. Do whatever it takes to experience more of Jesus.

Be Amazing!

As mentioned in the Introduction, I want Jesus to look at me like the Roman centurion and say "I haven't seen faith like Matthew Hartsfield's in all of Tampa Bay!" That is my goal, to thrill and amaze the heart of Jesus with my absolute faith and trust in him. I hope that's your goal too! Don't you want to amaze Jesus every day with a sold out faith that won't settle for anything less than God's best?

> Don't you want to amaze Jesus every day with a sold out faith that won't settle for anything less than God's best?

Like the centurion, we have to acknowledge Jesus has full authority in the spiritual realm. We are spiritual beings, and that means Jesus has full authority over us at all times. The only question for us is whether we will surrender to that authority and cooperate with it. We are encouraged by our culture to "question authority." While this may be fine with our secular authorities, it will never move us into the deeper places with Jesus. I must give my unquestioning allegiance to Jesus and trust his control. Jesus said, *"If you love me, obey my commandments"* (John 14:15).

The Roman centurion obeyed his superior officers out of obligatory duty and fear. Likewise, his soldiers obeyed him for the same reasons. But Jesus said to obey his commandments out of love. Have you ever fully loved someone you couldn't fully trust? It's impossible. If I am going to completely love Jesus I have to completely trust him. I want to have amazing faith in Jesus because ultimately I want to have amazing love for Jesus. So, by amazing Jesus with my faith I am also amazing him with my love! Be amazing to Jesus!

11.

GO AGAINST ALL ODDS

Large crowds followed Jesus as
he came down the hillside. Look!
A leper is approaching. He kneels
before him, worshiping. "Sir,"
the leper pleads, "if you want to,
you can heal me." Jesus touches
the man. "I want to," he says. "Be
healed." And instantly the
leprosy disappears.
Matthew 8:1–3 (TLB)

Jesus was delivering his famous "Sermon on the Mount." Many were in the crowd that day, swarming around this mysterious new Rabbi. They were listening intently, amazed at the authority and wisdom of his words. But one person in the crowd that day listened with the greatest intensity of all. He also listened impatiently. Most people like it when a preacher says "In conclusion," but this man had been waiting years for this moment!

He had remained as hidden as possible in the midst of the crowd. He tried to cover his face and hands. He didn't want anybody to notice his presence until he was ready to make his move. But why all the secrecy? Why remain hidden in this swarm of people?

This man suffered from the dreaded skin disease of leprosy. According to Luke's gospel, he was in an advanced stage of the disease (Luke 5:12). Because of his contagious state, this man would have been cut off from all normal contact with people. He was considered "unclean." Most people considered his disease God's punishment for some great sin in his life.

Most likely he lived outside the town, possibly with other lepers in a community set aside for these outcasts. He would have been shunned from family, friends, even from worship in the synagogue. Many lepers were made to wear little bells that would signal their presence so others could steer clear. Other regulations required them to yell "unclean" if they were passing anywhere near "normal" people (Leviticus 13:45,46). Lepers were basically the poster children for hopelessness.

But something inside this leper still clung tenaciously to hope. Something kept him going. Something kept his dreams of a normal life alive. That something was someone—Jesus. This leper knew he had to see Jesus that day. He had to get near his healing power. He had to approach Jesus against all odds. It would mean risking his life, whatever was left of it.

That's why this man had to "suddenly" approach Jesus. If people in the crowd knew a leper had mingled among them unannounced they could have stoned him! So, at the conclusion of Jesus' message the man jockeyed for position to get right in front of the Rabbi. Jesus deserved to take a well-earned break when the leper rudely thrust himself into Jesus' path.

Oddly enough, in this mad rush to Jesus, the leper didn't immediately make a request for healing. He began by getting on his knees, worshipping Jesus as Lord. He let Jesus know he trusted not only in his power, but in his purpose, saying, *"if you want to, you can make me well again."*

The crowd was shocked, stunned and silent. The scene was about to turn bad for the leper, real bad. Jesus, however, acted first. Many in the crowd expected words of rebuke. The Rabbi would certainly react with indignation and anger. Instead, Jesus reacted in a way that brought even greater shock to the stunned onlookers. Mark's gospel tells us Jesus was *"moved with pity"* (Mark 1:41). In the original Greek language that phrase means that Jesus was moved deep in his gut over the plight of this man.

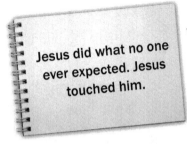

Jesus did what no one ever expected. Jesus touched him.

Jesus' first reaction was unexpected. He did not rebuke or heal. His first reaction went beyond mere words. Jesus did what no one ever expected. Jesus touched him. He touched him!

For years this man had gone without the simple pleasure of human touch. What others took for granted he could only dream of feeling. He hadn't felt the grip of a friend's handshake in years. For too long he hadn't felt the warmth of his wife's hug. And it seemed like forever since he had shared an embrace with his children.

Jesus knew that, more than anything else, this man simply needed to be touched. And while this man was melting in the warmth of Jesus' touch, Jesus spoke the actual words of healing. The words were almost secondary, an afterthought. In the instant Jesus touched him, he knew healing was on its way!

Hope Anyway

Everything in the leper's life reminded him he was "hopeless." Each day was a reinforcement of his physical, emotional and spiritual pain. Long ago this man should have thrown in the towel. Why hope? Why dream? Why even live anymore?

Jesus specializes in hopeless causes. Each story we have seen demonstrates how much Jesus desires to stir hope in the hopeless. From Genesis to Revelation God reminds us He loves to make a way where there seems to be no way. Just look at the track record of

Jesus specializes in hopeless causes.

restored hope in the stories of people God used in mighty ways against all odds. Sarah and Abraham were too old (Genesis 21). Jeremiah was too young (Jeremiah 1). Isaiah was too sinful (Isaiah 6). Jonah was too scared (Jonah 1). Moses was too stubborn (Exodus 4 & 5). Peter was too impulsive (John 13:38, 18:10-27). Thomas was too doubtful (John 20:24-25). Paul was too hateful (Acts 8). Lazarus was too dead (John 11).

Can you add your name to the list? What causes you to lose hope? Like the leper, what makes you feel frustrated, isolated or beyond God's touch? Sometimes we have no human reason to hold onto hope. But we don't need any human reasons. We need Jesus. St. Teresa of Avila wrote, "Let nothing disturb thee, let nothing dismay thee. All things pass; God never changes."[1]

God, speaking through the mouthpiece of the prophet Isaiah, reminds us of this.

> *Don't be afraid, for I have*
> *ransomed you; I have called you*
> *by name; you are mine. When you*
> *go through deep waters and great*
> *trouble, I will be with you. When*
> *you go through rivers of difficulty,*
> *you will not drown! When you walk*
> *through the fire of oppression, you*
> *will not be burned up—the flames*
> *will not consume you. For I am the*
> *Lord, your God, your Savior, the*
> *Holy One of Israel."*
> Isaiah 43:1–3 (TLB)

Suddenly Approach

The leper knew he was taking his life into his hands. He knew his approach was a bold move. In fact, his sudden approach to Jesus was a rude move!

---

1   Peers, E. Allison, editor *"Poem IX"*, *Complete Works St. Teresa of Avila,* 1963, Vol. 3, p. 288.

Like most of the people we've seen so far, this man shouldn't have been anywhere near the Rabbi. He broke every convention of culture. He disregarded every rule of religious law. He dismissed the thoughts of the crowd. He was going to do whatever it took to get to Jesus.

He was, in fact, bothering Jesus. Jesus deserved a break. He had just finished a long and exhausting sermon. I know how tired I am after I step down from preaching a typical message. I can only imagine how Jesus must have felt after delivering the Sermon on the Mount! But this man does not act politely or consider Jesus' feelings. He simply and suddenly approaches Jesus, desperate and convinced that Jesus was the only answer to his problems.

So what's stopping you? Go ahead. Go for it. Take a risk. Bother Jesus! And do it suddenly. What are you waiting for? Bring your life, your dreams, your problems and your hopes to Jesus. Like the leper, trust his reaction will be one of compassion and not of criticism.

So what's stopping you? Go ahead. Go for it. Take a risk. Bother Jesus!

Approach on Your Knees

It's fascinating that this leper's first move was not a request for healing. His first move was worship. Before he said anything he got on his knees and gave Jesus honor and glory, calling him "Lord." How often do we approach Jesus without first affirming his lordship in our lives? Do we begin our time with God with a grocery list of demands, or do we get on our knees and humble ourselves in his presence?

Even though the leper "bothered" Jesus and broke all the rules, he did so with an attitude of humility and expectant worship. Jesus was moved with compassion because he discerned this man's heart. He knew the genuineness in this man's soul. He sensed the authentic desperation in this man's heart. His worship was real and he was willing to get on his knees before Jesus before anything else. If we are looking for God to show up in dramatic ways in our lives, we must be willing to show up in dramatic ways for God.

The Bible tells us God is looking for worshippers. God is actually scanning the globe, looking to reward true hearts of worship.

> *The eyes of the Lord search the whole earth in order to strengthen those whose hearts are fully committed to him.*
> 2 Chronicles 16:9

Don't you want a strengthened heart? God is clear he will bring strength to those who have committed their lives to his purposes. That's what true worship is all about. Worship is not just showing up on Sunday morning. Worship is not just singing songs. Worship is not just reciting creeds. I know how easy it is for me to want to place God in a box called church and keep my worship safe and tame in that little box. But that's not true worship.

Worship is about a whole-life commitment to the things of God. We worship God at work. We worship God at play. We worship God with our thoughts and attitudes. We worship God in our giving. We worship God in our serving. We worship God in our prayers. We worship God in our Bible reading.

This leper had a heart that was sold out to Jesus and he was willing risk his life to show it. He was willing to get on his knees to demonstrate it. He was willing to reveal his vulnerable heart to Jesus. What are you willing to do? To what lengths will you go to worship Jesus with a humble, expectant heart? We all need the desperate heart of a leper to worship like that!

12.

RUN THROUGH REJECTIONS

One day some parents brought
their children to Jesus so he could
lay his hands on them and pray for
them. But the disciples scolded
the parents for bothering him. But
Jesus said, "Let the children come
to me. Don't stop them! For the
Kingdom of Heaven belongs to
those who are like these children."
And he placed his hands on their
heads and blessed them
before he left.
Matthew 19:13-15

Jesus left Galilee, heading south into Judea, east of the Jordan River. But no matter where he went the masses of people were now an ever present reality. Vast crowds swarmed him. It was a constant blur of people. The disciples were growing weary of all the commotion. And now, to make matters worse, parents were bringing their children for Jesus to bless.

Enough is enough! This was the last straw for the disciples. It was one thing for the adults to crowd around Jesus and make demands on him. But now these little kids were running around, trying to get next to Jesus. Didn't they know this was no place for kids? Weren't they aware the Rabbi was too important to be bothered by these little rug rats?

The disciples decided to take matters into their own hands. Someone had to protect Jesus and serve as a screener for him. These disciples had already seen too many people rudely approach Jesus and bother him with all their unending needs! So these self-appointed bodyguards began to reject these little children, rebuking them for daring to bother the Master. Certainly they were doing Jesus a great favor. Later, in a precious moment of privacy, Jesus would certainly thank them for keeping these little kids away from him while he was engaged in his important work.

But the disciples were chagrined when Jesus cut them off and asked for all the kids to come to him. "Don't stop them," he said, motioning for the children to gather around him and climb up in his lap. The disciples felt rather sheepish as the children ran through and around them to get to Jesus. And not only did Jesus make way for the kids, he actually laid hands on their heads and spent time giving them each a blessing!

On top of all this, Jesus even went further by claiming that everyone had to become like these little children in order to enter the Kingdom of Heaven! Jesus was asking the disciples and the other followers to be like children? This was unheard of, and the disciples were left once again scratching their heads and pondering the words of this amazing Rabbi.

Don't Listen to the Rejections

Once again, someone is bothering Jesus. The disciples were simply being realistic and level-headed about the whole deal. But Jesus defied their human logic and once again rewarded the "botherers." These children and their parents were in the process of being rejected when Jesus intervened. Jesus told them to run past the rejections and come into his lap. When everyone was saying "Go away," Jesus spoke up and said, *"Come on in!"*

> When everyone was saying "Go away," Jesus spoke up and said, "Come on in!"

Ever felt like that? You know when the walls are up and the rejections are fast and furious. At times we feel like there is a barrier between us and Jesus—a barrier that seems as impenetrable as the big disciples were to the little children. We want the touch of Jesus. We want the blessing. We are seeking him but things and people keep getting in our way.

I'm sure the disciples seemed like giants to the little kids. Most adults don't realize how huge we seem to little eyes. Sometimes the obstacles we face in our lives appear as giants to us. We can't see past them and we wonder why we're not feeling the embrace of Jesus. Why does it seem like his lap, his embrace, his hand of blessing is so far away?

Regardless of the rejection we may be encountering in our lives, Jesus is always calling us to come and feel the touch of his blessing. Jesus is inviting you to come to him and enjoy his love. He is inviting you to come to him as a little child.

Go Ahead, Act Childish

Why would Jesus want us to become like children? The Apostle Paul wrote: *"But when I grew up, I put away childish things"* (1 Corinthians 13:11). Doesn't the Bible tell us to "grow" in Christ and strive for spiritual maturity? So what's up with the call to be a child?

Being a child means being dependent, vulnerable and trusting. Children count on parents and responsible adults in their lives for food, shelter, protection, love and encouragement. Children thrive best when they are in the care of loving and supportive parents who give all of themselves to that precious relationship. God wants us to recognize our complete and total dependence on him as our Heavenly Father—a loving, caring, protective father. Unless we are able to be children, we can't ever know God as Father. Unless we recognize our dependence on God we will never know all the love God has for us, his children.

This is why Jesus said to Nicodemus, *"So don't be surprised at my statement that you must be born again"* (John 3:7 TLB). Obviously, we have been born first as children of our biological parents. But in order to claim God as our Father we must allow ourselves to be symbolically born again, to be children again. In fact, we must be willing to put ourselves up for adoption. Paul reminds us:

> *Even before he made the world,*
> *God loved us and chose us in*
> *Christ to be holy and without fault*
> *in his eyes. 5 God decided in*
> *advance to adopt us into his own*
> *family by bringing us to himself*
> *through Jesus Christ. This is what*
> *he wanted to do, and it gave him*
> *great pleasure.*
> Ephesians 1:4–5

And this gave him great pleasure! As an adoptive parent God doesn't get "stuck" with us. Adoption means choice. God

> **As an adoptive parent God doesn't get "stuck" with us.**

chooses you! But he doesn't force his choice on you. You are invited to choose God's gift of his Son, Jesus Christ. You are invited to bring your brokenness to the only one who can give you wholeness. You are invited to lay down your anxiety and stress to the only one who can offer you peace. You are invited to receive forgiveness of your sins through Christ's sacrifice on the cross. You are invited to follow Jesus and discover the abundant life in this world and assurance of your heavenly home in eternity. You are invited to surrender to Jesus as Lord and Savior and become a precious and highly valued son or daughter of God the Father.

Best of all, God is not a parent in name only who simply feels some obligatory duty to take care of his children. It brings God great joy to adopt us as his sons and daughters, lavishing love on those who find their relationship with him through Jesus Christ. God loves being your father! And your relationship with God as Father gives you extreme comfort and confidence to approach him with wild abandon.

When my two daughters were small children they had a wonderful habit of running to the door to greet me whenever I entered the house. No matter where they were or what they were doing, they would drop it all to come running to me, jumping up into my waiting arms, ready to give me the biggest squeeze their little arms could offer. When they became teenagers I didn't get quite the same greeting (sigh).

And when my girls were growing up they regarded me as a great fount of wisdom. Their mother and I were often sought out to help them and assist them. They also came to us with any joy in their lives. They wanted to share their experiences with us. Again, when they became teenagers I was no longer the great source of knowledge. Did you notice Jesus didn't say: "Let the *teenagers* come to me. Don't stop them! For the Kingdom of Heaven belongs to such as these."

If I, as an earthly father, feel such joy from my children running to me, then how much more must God feel as our Heavenly Father? And if I derive great satisfaction when my girls come to me for help and advice, I can only imagine how much God must love it when I come to him and ask for his direction and guidance. Sometimes God must feel like the parent of teenagers. We all delude ourselves into a belief that we know everything and don't need our Heavenly Father.

When was the last time you sought out God's advice as a trusting child approaching a loving father? When was the last time you came running to God like a little kid, ready to jump up into the his waiting arms, giving your father a huge squeeze! This is the invitation we have in Jesus Christ. We are invited to come as little children, boldly running past all of the rejection, pain, hurt, regret and resentments in our lives as we throw ourselves into the lap of our Heavenly Father.

*...let us go right into the presence
of God, with true hearts fully
trusting him.*

Hebrews 10:22

CLOSING CHALLENGE

When I was unpacking each of these stories, I had to stop and do a little self-diagnosis. I surprised myself. I finished each chapter both comforted and disturbed. I felt like I was writing to myself and letting you read over my shoulder. Left unchecked, I tend to veer toward what's safe, predictable and controlled. I confess, I want God to conform to my image and play by my rules. But that makes for a small God and an even smaller me.

How about you? Are you ready to stop being so polite? Is it time to start enjoying a relationship with God that's a little more raw and unrestrained? Are you ready to unleash your faith?

Unleashing your faith means taking off the self-imposed limitations that keep you from experiencing all the best of Jesus. In what ways have you  kept your faith on a leash? Where have you lowered your expectations, dialed down your dreams or diminished your hopes?

Sometimes we keep our faith on a leash because we're scared. Or all too often we keep it restrained because we've been let down before and we don't want to get our hopes up again.

But most of us keep our faith tied up because we never really understood how awesome and unleashed God's love is for us! That's right! God's love for you is unleashed. He is extravagantly in love with you and wants you to experience the best of him.

Maybe the best way to unleash your love for God is to realize how much he is already head-over-heels in love with you. When you know how much someone unconditionally loves you, it is a lot easier to fully trust and surrender to that person. You would do anything to connect with that person, anything to spend time with that person.

So what are you waiting for?

- Go climb a tree.
- Dig a hole.
- Scream in the storm.
- Start begging.
- Claw through crowds.
- Sneak through darkness.
- Keep on asking.
- Push beyond boundaries.
- Go against all odds.
- Run through rejections.

ABOUT THE AUTHOR

Matthew Hartsfield is the Senior Pastor of Van Dyke Church in Lutz, Florida, one of the largest and fastest growing United Methodist Churches in America. He has served there since 1993. Matthew graduated from Nova Southeastern University in 1984 with a B.S. in Psychology. He earned his Master of Divinity Degree at Emory University in 1987. From there he served as Associate Pastor at Southside United Methodist Church in Jacksonville, Florida from 1987 to 1989. He then served as Senior Pastor at The First United Methodist Church in Lake Alfred, Florida from 1989 to 1993.

Matthew's passion has always been to help people connect in meaningful and life-changing ways to God's Word. Through his preaching and other speaking engagements, he helps the Bible come alive in people's minds and hearts. He has a teacher's heart and wants people to know and apply the powerful truths from Scripture.

Matthew is married to Maisie and they have two grown daughters, Sarah and Jill.

You can follow Matthew on his blog at www.MatthewHartsfield.com.

Made in the USA
Charleston, SC
01 February 2012